# SRIM

**B.K. Chaturvedi**

All rights reserved. No part of this book may be reproduced, stored in a retrieval system or transmitted in any form, electronic, mechanical, photocopying, recording or otherwise without prior written permission from the publisher.

**ISBN: 81-7182-831-0**

**© Publisher**

| | |
|---|---|
| Published by | : **Diamond Pocket Books (P) Ltd.** X-30, Okhla Industrial Area, Phase-II New Delhi-110020 |
| Phone | : 011-41611861 |
| Fax | : 011-41611866 |
| E-mail | : sales@diamondpublication.com |
| Website | : www.dpb.in |
| Edition | : 2006 |
| Price | : Rs. 95/- US $ 7/- |
| Printed by | : Adarsh Printers, Navin Shahdara, Delhi-110032 |

**Srimad Bhagwat Puran**
by *B.K. Chaturvedi* — Rs. 95/-

# Preface

The 'Srimad Bhagwat' itself is believed to be the gem among all the sacred Puranas as it emphasises on the devotion to Lord Vishnu's incarnation, Lord Krishna. It is believed to have been authored by the great sage Vedavyasa when he felt a great unrest troubling his soul after authoring the Mahabharat. Although this Purana itself is believed to be a part of Skanda Purana, it is its lyrical beauty and devotion to Krishna that made it most popular. It enlists 22 incarnations of Lord Vishnu, while other sacred accounts of the Sanatana Dharma believe that there were nine incarnations and one is yet to come.

Normally in the Purana, the tales or stories frequently overlap with each other giving emphasis on a different point. Owing to paucity of space, many of the stories have been given a brief mention in this work with the footnote guiding to the sources, to get the full story in the other Puranas. There are also certain variations in the details of the stories which have been also marked within parenthesis. Also, many details mentioned in this Puran which may appear uninteresting, have been deliberately left out. Some of the stories which are well-known have been skipped. For example, the Ramakatha or the details about other incarnations popularised by other sacred sources. The main emphasis in culling out the stories has been on those stories that reveal the basic moral fiber of our ethos.

These stories have been recreated keeping in mind the comprehension of our young learners and hence making these stories more logical. This work is only an attempt to make our society recapture its roots. That is why the language and style have been used with great care so as to make the stories readable and comprehensive.

It is hoped that our discerning readership will accord it a warm welcome. Lastly, the author wishes to record his gratitude to Narenderji of Diamond Pocket Books whose crusade to publish the gems of our cultural and religious ethos has few parallels in the field of publishing.

B.K. Chaturvedi

## Contents

1. The Great Glory of Shrimadbhagwat ......... 7
2. The Creation of The Srimad Bhagwat ......... 12
3. The Descent of this Grand Puran to Common People ......... 15
4. Shukadeva Recites This Purana Before Parikshit ......... 17
5. The Description of The Various Incarnations of The Blessed Lord ......... 24
6. Brahma Starts The Process of Creation ......... 27
7. Sage Kardem Helps in The Process of Creation ......... 30
8. The Progeny of Manu's Daughters ......... 32
9. Daksha's Hostility for Shiva And Sati's Death By Self-Immolation ......... 33
10. The Sun's Transitional Phase and Speed of Movement ......... 36
11. The Tale of Priyavrata ......... 38
12. The Tale of Raja Prithu ......... 40
13. Ajaamil's Salvation ......... 44
14. Rishabha Deva and Jada-Bharat ......... 46
15. The Dwarf (Vamana) Incarnation ......... 48
16. Shiva Falls for Mohini ......... 52
17. Lord Hari Saves The Elephant, Gajendra Moksha ......... 55
18. The Story of Naabhag And Ambreesha ......... 64
19. King Dushyanta And Bharata ......... 67
20. Raja Rantideo's Hospitality ......... 70
21. The Descent of The Ganga ......... 71
22. Marriage of Vasudeva And Devaki ......... 74
23. Incarnation of Lord Krishna And Other Events ......... 76
24. Kansa Dethroned And Destroyed ......... 85
25. Krishna Outwits Brahma ......... 87
26. Krishna and Balrama Feel Hungry ......... 89
27. The Emancipation of Vidyadhara Sudarshana ......... 91

| | | |
|---|---|---|
| 28. | Akroora's Confusion Dispelled | 93 |
| 29. | Krishna And Kubja | 95 |
| 30. | Krishna Meets His Parents For The First Time | 97 |
| 31. | Jarasandha Attacks Mathura | 99 |
| 32. | Krishna Sends Uddhava To Vraja | 102 |
| 33. | Krishna Marries Rukmini | 105 |
| 34. | Kamdeva Regains His Body in the Form of Pradyumna | 108 |
| 35. | The Syamantak Mani (Gem) Episode | 110 |
| 36. | Shalva Attacks Dwarika | 113 |
| 37. | Krishna Beheads Shishupal | 115 |
| 38. | Krishna Kills Narakasura And Releases The Helpless Women | 117 |
| 39. | Krishna And Balarama Pay Their Guru's Fees | 119 |
| 40. | Sudama And Krishna | 122 |
| 41. | Yashoda and Krishna's Reunion | 125 |
| 42. | Arjuna Marries Subhadra | 127 |
| 43. | A Strange Fact | 129 |
| 44. | Devaki Gets Back Her Six Dead Sons | 131 |
| 45. | Bhasmasur Destroyed | 132 |
| 46. | Who Among The Super Gods Is The Greatest? | 134 |
| 47. | Arjuna Purged of His Arrogance | 136 |
| 48. | Lord Krishna Contemplates About Quitting the Mortal World | 139 |
| 49. | The Twenty Four 'Gurus' of Dattatreya | 141 |
| 50. | The Details About Lord Krishna's Family | 147 |
| 51. | The End of the Yadava Clan | 149 |
| 52. | Lord Krishna Departs For His Eternal Abode | 151 |
| 53. | The Dynasties In Kaliyug | 153 |
| 54. | The Description of The Final Dissolution or Pralaya | 156 |
| 55. | Raja Parikshit's Salvation And Janmejaya's 'Naag-Yaga' | 158 |

# 1

# The Great Glory of Shrimadbhagwat

Long long ago, there lived a very religious and pious brahmin named, Atmadeva on the bank of the river Tungbhadra. He was a rich man and had a beautiful wife called Dhundhuli. Although the brahmin had every happiness, yet he had no son. This was enough reason to make him feel sad all the time. Despite being garrulous, his wife cared for his every comfort. But Atmadeva remained always grief striken with the thought: "Who will be my prop in the old age? Who'd offer liberation to me and my dead ancestors when I will be gone? I would thus be failing in my duty to my departed ancestors. Really a son-less life is hell. Shouldn't I quit it?" And one day in the fit of emotion, he departed to the woods, leaving his wife all alone.

When he reached deep in the woods, he had no idea about the direction. He was feeling thirsty. After a hard search he could spot a pond that was rather far-off. With great difficulty he did manage to reach it, but exhaustion made him collapse near the pond. He fell down and began to cry.

At that very moment, a brilliant hermit happend to pass that spot. Hearing him, he came close and asked: "You look very much a brahmin with a holy mark on your forehead and the sacred thread upon your shoulder. But why do you cry?"

Atmadeva, then, told him the tale of his woe and lamented "Sir! A life without a son is hell for a noble brahmin like me, always desiring to pay his due to the departed ancestors. But I'm so unfortunate, that let alone my wife conceiving a son for me, even the cow in my house stays barren."

The hermit looked at his face and said: "Dear! Provident hasn't ordained a son for you. Forget about it and go to the forest to meditate and remember God."

"But what about my familial obligation?" Atmadeva questioned, adding: "Should I be devoting my attention to God when my ancestors are thirsty?"

At this the brilliant ascetic felt pity on Atmadeva. After thinking for a while the ascetic said: "Now I have made a special prayer for you. Take this fruit and make your wife eat it. As soon as you planted your seed into her, she would get a son for you."

Atmadeva was delighted getting this boon. Happily he returned home and made his wife eat the fruit, as he was advised. When Dhundhali heard the efficacious consequence of her eating that fruit, she was unwilling to eat: "I want a son all right but I don't want my body to get disfigured in the process. Moreover, then I would have to rear up that child and do all the dirty jobs for his comfort. I don't want to go through that mess."

As her luck would have it, at that very time there happened to reach her cousin. When Dhundhali showed her the fruit and confided her quandary into her, her sister said: "Well! I am pregnant. If you give me good money may be, I will sell my would-be child to you, should he be a boy."

The deal was struck. The Dhundhali said: "But we must also test the potency of this fruit. Let my cow eat it. She is also pregnant." At due time, Dhundhali received clandestinely the new born boy from her sister, while Atmadeva was all unaware of all these tidings. Exactly at that time the cow also delivered a human baby, who had his whole body like a boy barring for the ears, which were typically like that of a cow. At due time, Atmadeva had the name ceremony of the two children solemised. The son of Atmadeva and Dhundhali was called Dhundhukari and the boy from the cow called Gokarna (literally meaning one with a cow like ears).

Immediately after the 'supposed' delivery of the boy Dhundhukari, Dhundhali complained of not getting milk in her breast for the child's feeding. So, on her request, Atmadeva agreed to call her that sister, who had also delivered a son who, she claimed, died at his very birth. The unsuspecting brhamin, Atmadeva, believed all his wife told him. At last, that woman was called to feed Dhundhukari who was, in fact the boy's real mother.

Both the boys began to grow together. Although Gokarna emerged to be a noble, religious, God-fearing brahmin but Dhundhukari, right from the beginning, emerged as a rogue. The latter had no good sanskaras. So he mired into evil habits like stealing, setting fire to the houses of innocent without any provocation, throwing little kids in the well and indulging in armed fighting with his fellow beings. He always moved in the company of dogs and never hesitated to commit even the most heinous crimes.

Eventually, he turned out to be a pest to his own family. He started torturing his parents for getting money to gamble and visit prostitutes. He troubled them so much that Atmadeva even cried once to exclaim: "Oh! We were any time better without any male issue. My son is actually a demon."

Gokarna heard his cry this way. He advised his foster father: "You are learned enough to know that in this world no relation is true or permanent. Why are your trapped in this worthless frustration for son and family? You should go to forest and meditate on God—who provides succour to all." Atmadeva heeded to his advise and left his home and family finally for the woods. Now Dhundhukari started torturing his mother for money. At last, when she couldn't put up with his torture, she jumped into a blind well to end her life.

Now, the rogue Dhundhukari had a free play. He brought four prostitutes and began to stay in that house. The nautch-girls never loved him and they only wanted money. One day, when Dhundhukari was left with no money, the four wicked women jointly tied him and beat him as much as, to eventually end Dhundhukari's life. After gathering all the costly items in the house, they left.

Meanwhile, Gokarna continued to become a respectable and erudite member of the society. He had completed his pilgrimage to all the holy spots. When he returned home, he found it empty since by that time the inmates of the house-his father, mother and brother—had either been killed or gone to the jungle. Finding the house totally vacant, he decided to re-establish it with the help of the local villagers.

Dhundhukari was also staying in that house in the form of a ghost.

Since his death took place much before the due time, he had become a ghost. Seeing his brother back he started troubling him by creating horrible images during the nights. Now he would adopt the form of a buffalo, or of a deadly boar to frighten his brother Gokarna. But Gokarna was a religious person, chanting the holy Gayatri Mantra every day in the morning after bath. So he was beyond the projection of all the ill spectacles brought by any ghost. However, he realised that there was an evil spirit troubling him. So, he chanted a Mantra and sprinkled holy water on that figure of ghost. The ghost became some what subdued with the effect of that Mantra and got back his power to communicate in a human language. He supplicated before Gokarna "O brother! please do something to have me released from this ghostly existence. I'm really a wicked soul, since I troubled every one I came in contact with. Although I am suffering the consequences of my evil deeds, yet, for old time's sake, I request you to help me."

Gokarna was amazed to find his brother Dhundhukari in this form. "But why was your soul not released when I performed your Shraddha in Gaya as well? I had learnt about your death from our father who was then meditating in the forest, closeby."

"Mere Shraddha won't be able to liberate my soul, brother, as it is steeped in filth and sin. You will have to make a special prayer to release my soul."

Assuring him to do something about it, Gokarna went to consult his seniors in the village. The learned scholars suggested: "Only our devoted worship to Sun-God may help, as he knows every secret of this world he circumambulates around."

At last, their faithful worship to Sun-God made the deity appear before them to advise, "Only a devoted chanting of the holy Puran, Srimad Bhagwat, can help your wicked brother. If his ghost listens to this holy discourse fully and faithfully, he may get the due release."

Getting this advice, the learned scholars asked Gokarna to start reading aloud the Srimad Bhagwat. Since Gokarna was a renowned man, an erudite scholar and a very pious being, thousands of persons assembled to hear this highly auspicious Purana from Gokarna's mouth.

Gokarna had also advised Dhundhuakari to reach the venue of the holy recital. But how could a ghost stay amidst the living beings? After much effort, the ghost could find an empty bamboo pole having seven joints. He secretly occupied his place inside it and began to listen to the Puran. When the first pause to the chanting of that holy text came, the people saw an unusual spectacle. As the recitation ended the top joint of the bamboo burst with a loud noise. Then with every pause in the seven-day long recital, the joints of the bamboo kept on bursting till the final, seventh day, when the whole bamboo had burst out, signifying the final release of the ghost Dhundhukari's soul. This way Gokarna made his wicked brother's soul get a respectable liberation. Then Gokarna kept on reciting the holy Puran before thousands of people for years together. When his time came, a divine Vimana (aerial vehicle) came to escort him alive to the most noble heaven, Vaikuntha.

This story highlights the fact that the recitation of this holy Bhagwat can make the person highly pious and get a berth in the heaven. No other Purana is believed to be as holy and as auspicious to liberate, even the most wicked soul.

◻◻

# 2
## The Creation of The Srimad Bhagwat

As we all know, each Manavanter has a Vedavyas to properly edit and compile the available knowledge. In the present Manavanter, the Vedavyas was Shree Krishna Dweipayan. He was an illegitmate son of the sage Parashar and Satyavati, a daughter of the head of the boatman living on the bank of the river Yamuna, near Indraprastha.

He was a very precocious child and soon he acquired mastery over all knowledge. In accordance with the boon that he received from his father, Parashar, left his mother to pursue his studies and in no time, became as much deft as, to claim authority over every branch of knowledge.

One day, he heard a divine voice guiding him to compile and edit all the knowledge that was available then. He took up this enormous job. He divided the basic knowledge in four parts and called each part, a Veda. Having done so, he classified the remaining knowledge in the form of various Puranas and Upanishadas.

In order to facilitate their easier comprehension, he abridged all that knowledge into a huge compendium called the Mahabharat. He earned a great acclaim for having accomplished this enormous task for the benefit of the entire human race. All the kings and emperors honoured the sage Vedavyas. He appeared satisfied with his work yet he was not happy at heart. Since while writing the Mahabharat he had to consider every depravity that could afflict the human brain, he became quite desolate realising how mean a human mind could become. Moreover, he found that despite his proper editing of all the available sacred texts, his heart developed a growing aversion for even the human existence.

One day, he was sitting on the bank of the river Saraswati, quite desolate and forlorn seeing the world becoming increasingly unrighteous and vile. "Still the people are unhappy and sad. Even though, they now have the sacred text made comprehensible even for the most lower stratum of the society, they don't go by the Vedic dictum and indulge in all kinds of vile persuits. What is the purpose of having all these teachings available, when the people don't abide by them? What should I do to make them drawn to the righteous path and get, in the process, some happiness for my own heart torn with the realisation of the lowly levels, that a man can stoop to serve his heinous selfish ends? In fact, having written the Mahabharat I now realise, how beastly can a man become? Are there no means by which a human society could experience a divine attitude and a real solace to its heart?"

While he was lost in his thought, his reverie was broken, all of a sudden with the melodious chant of "Narayana-Narayana". When he looked up, he found the divine sage, Narad, before him. "Why are you sitting in such a pensive mood, O sage! What is making you look so desolate and dissatisfied? Aren't you satisfied with the great work you have already accomplished?"

Vedavyas welcomed the sage and confided in him all that was troubling his heart. Narad heard him patiently for ten days long. Next day, when both of them had finished their daily chores including ritual worship, Narad accosted Vedavyas: "O Master of the Vedas and all the sacred knowledge, I have identified the main cause that rankles your heart. While in writing all these masterly treaties, you taxed your mind undoubtedly, that you could do nothing that could make your heart attain bliss and beautitude to satisfy your soul. While you delved deeply into the realm of reason, you have not even touched faith. Remember that it is never the reason but the faith that sublimates one's soul. Now you should write something that goes straight into the heart. Write about Lord Krishna, the Rasaraj, the respository of all delights of heart, the acme and aim of all devotion. Only when you recreate his childhood pranks, his youthful dalliance and his 'Virat-Purush' (the prime person) like-doings, that not only your heart will get the much-needed contentment but all the people of the world too would get a source to receive the solace of the soul."

Vedavyas detected a ray of light in the allround enveloping darkness. "So shall I do", he promised to the divine sage. Then Narada left for Brahma's realm and Vedavyas began the preparations to take up the project to lighten his soul. Since most of the events of Lord Krishna's life he had personally witnessed, it took him no time to write the auspicious and holy 'Srimad Bhagwat' for the delight of the entire human race.

◻◻

# 3

# The Descent of this Grand Puran to Common People

Once at the holy spot of Nemisharanya, assembled all the learned seers and sages at the end of the Kali Age, including the brilliant saint Shaunak. They all reventially welcomed the Soota Ji[1] and requested him: "O Esteemed Sage! You have learnt all history, science, logic and the theoretical details of our ancient lore. We now request you to tell us, as to how Vyas Ji created the Bhagwat Puran and who were the persons who listened to it in totality?"

The Soota Ji said: "Narad's advice made Vedavyas quite enthusiastic to create this Puran centered on Lord Vishnu's most potent incarnation, Lord Krishna's life event. When he had composed he thought it, "Now who should be the first to listen to it from me? I don't want any undeserving person to come even close to it, let alone listen to its contents."

While he was thinking thus, he suddenly realised that Shukadeva, his son, should be the most deserving one as he was totally free from worldly lust and infatuation with no trace of guile, even in his heart."

To emphasise upon Shukadeva's virtues, Sootaji recounted an episode: "Once Sage Vedavyas and Shukadeva were passing from a nearby pond, in which the divine beauties (Apsaras) were having their merry bath. As they approached, seeing first the sage Vyas, the danseuse quickly came out of the pond and cover their almost unclad bodies with proper clothes. Vyas Ji was rather surprised to find,

---

[1]. Literally, the narrator but in this context the learned sage who knew all the sacred texts very well.

the Apsaras continuing their merry bath, when Shukadeva, following him, passed from that very point. "It is really amazing that these young divine beauties took so much care to hide their, almost uncovered bodies, seeing an old man like me, approach them. But when they saw a young person, my son Shukadeva, come closer, they didn't care to hide their unclad bodies? This was despite the fact that a young male would be more titillated, by seeing their unclad bodies than an old man like me. Why did they do so?"

Thinking this way, the sage Vyas couldn't help enquiring about this from Apsaras. And they gave him this matter-of-fact reply: "Pardon our saying so, but the fact is, O sage, that despite your erudition and supreme learning, you still react to such temptation, as the relish for the sensual delights is very much present in your mind.

"On the other hand" the Apsaras continued, "Your son, Shukadeva, is so pious that he is beyond any effect of such sensual titillations. Hence, we feel no shame in standing unclad before him, but we did feel shy to let you see us at that stage. Hence, our precaution before you."

The Apsara's interpretation made Vedavyas realise his shortcomings and further confirmed his opinion about his son being totally guileless and hence, the most deserving candidate to listen to the holy Puran, Srimad Bhagwat.

His opinion got further confirmed, when like a normal father Vedavyas asked Shukadeva to get married. But the wise son replied, "Sir! I always thought you to be a learned and erudite scholar but I think you are also getting carried away by emotions like a normal, mortal person. Don't the scriptures say, that all mortal relations are not permanent and the real one is only one with the Supereme Spirit."

So, after having confirmed his opinion about his son, he thought him to be the most deserving listener to his creation, Srimad Bhagwat. Shukadeva received this Mahapuran from his father.

◻◻

# 4

# Shukadeva Recites This Purana Before Parikshit

Shukadeva conveyed the gist of this Grand Puran to Parikshit when the latter was frightened due to a sage's curse. What caused the sage, to curse this reign of the Pandavas and the only survivor of the entire Kuru dynasty is revealed in the story given below:–

When on the 18th day of the Grand battle of Mahabharat even Shalya was killed, Duryodhan realised that now it was impossible to win this war against the Pandavas. Deeming his final defeat to be a foregone conclusion, in order to avoid his capture by the Pandavas, he chose to flee and hide himself inside a pond in a jungle, having stilled its water by his yogic power. Meanwhile, the Pandavas were searching for him. They learnt from a hunter about the whereabouts of the missing Kaurava prince. Soon they surrounded that pond and challanged Duryodhan to come out of the water and fight a duel with any of them. Duryodhan was a brave man, came out of the pond and chose to fight a duel with Bhim. Then started a fierce mace duel between the two warriors, but encouraged by the trick hinted by Lord Krishna, Bhim broke Duryodhan's both thighs. Having totally incapicitated him, they left him to die in that eerie jungle.

However, all was not lost for the Kauravas. Their three stalwarts (Maharathees) Kripacharya, Kritavarma and Aswatthama were very much alive. They kept hiding themselves in the same forest till the Pandavas left after incapacitating Duryodhan. As the night fell, they came out like the beasts from their hide-outs, and reached near their fallen king, Duryodhan, crying bitterly on seeing their king's sorry condition. Duryodhan himself consoled them and said: "Cry not, my warriors, for this must have been ordained in my fate. I am still grateful for all you have done for me and the care you took to come to me."

Ashwatthama, the youngest and the most brilliant archer among them, was not to be reconciled. He thundered: "Till you are alive you are my king. I shall teach those coward Pandavas a lesson for violating the war-laws to defeat you. I shall behead all of them." He was trembling with rage, while saying so. Seeing his mood, Duryodhan asked Kripacharya to appoint Ashwatthama as the last Commander-in-Chief of the Kaurava forces which, the one time Guru of the, Kauravas did. As Duryodhan appointed him with the consecrated water, Ashwatthama took an oath: "Now, I shall only return to my king, when I will have the five hacked off heads of the Pandavas as my souvenir to assert your ultimate victory."

Saying so, the threesome left. They went straight to the camp of the Pandavas and waited for the night to carry out their intentions in darkness. The day-long spying, had made them identify the royal tents where the Pandavas were staying. Ashwatthama thought that his job had become comparatively easy since, his all 'preys' were available in one tent only. He waited for the night-fall.

Meanwhile, on the advise of their priest, Dhaumya, the Pandavas, fortunately, decided to pass that night worshipping the Goddess in a sort of 'thanks-giving ceremony' for their now almost-assured victory over the Kauravas. Instead, the five sons of Draupadi were sleeping in the tent there, when at midnight Ashwatthama attacked them. Since the attack was sudden and tottally unexpected, the Pandava forces were taken by surprise. On the instructions of their newly appointed Commander-in-chief, Kripacharya and Kritvarma guarded the gate and slayed everyone, who tried to escape. Soon, Ashwathama, almost drenched in blood of his enemies, emerged at the gate with five heads gibbeted in a keen spear. Still he thought that those heads belonged to the Pandavas. Since it was dark, he couldn't identify them properly.Soon the threesome left for their king with their 'war-momentoes'.

"O king," a beaming Ashwatthama accosted his almost dead king, Duryodhan, "here are the hacked heads of your five sworn enemics."

"Really," exclaimed a delighted Duryodhan, feeling as if new life was getting infused in his almost dead body. "Give me first the head of Bhim. I want to crush it with my bare hands." As Kripacharya handed the desired head to Duryodhan, the latter crushed it between his hands and it broke. "This can't be the head of Bhim. It is too soft." By that time the glow of dawn had considerably brightened the surroundings. And when all of them watched the hacked heads closely, they detected the mistake. Draupadi's five sons were the last survivors of the second generation of the entire Kuru's clan.

Even Duryodhan uttered in grief: "O Guruputra! You have now wiped off our whole clan. There is no survivor to continue our lineage, even after the Pandavas." Exclaiming in grief Duryodhan passed away. Kripacharya also went back to his hermitage and Kritavarma hastely proceeded to his native place in Dwarika.

Now Ashwatthama was left alone. He knew that the Pandavas would not rest a minute after knowing what he had done. They would be there any time braying for his blood. So he also decided to escape. He changed his clothes, became a brahmin student and quietly joined a school, run by a sage, close by.

Meanwhile, the Pandavas searching for him went to every possible place, where Ashwattama could have been, and gathering clues, happened to surround the school. Ashwatthama tore a sturdy stem of a long grass and set it on his bow while charging it with the deadly Brahmastra.

Then he released it, aiming at the Pandavas with the exclamation: "Let the Pandavas be wiped from the surface of the earth". Meanwhile, when Arjuna saw Ashwatthama aiming a Brahmastra at them, he also invoked his divine weapon of the same name and released it with the exclamation: "Let my Guru's son get his due."

Seeing the two deadly weapons clashing amidst air, all the sages rushed to that spot detecting the clashing weapons springing deadly fire-lings. The Sage Vedavyas requested both, Arjuna and Ashwatthama, to withdraw their weapons.

While Arjuna could do so, Ashwatthama expressed his inability to do so. Then he was advised to have his weapon's energy released on a worthless object. And then, displaying his beastly venegeance, Ashwatthama guided his divine missile on to the womb of Uttara, the wife of Abhimanyu. She was pregnant and was likely to become the mother of the sole survivor of the Kuru's clan. In order to exterminate the whole lineage of the Pandavas, this savage, Ashwatthama, had shown his beastly erudity by destroying the embryo inside Uttara's womb. This enraged Lord Krishna, who was also there, to curse Ashwatthama. Infact, Ashwatthama was the only person Lord Krishna had ever cursed. The Lord thundered: "O Guru-Putra! You commit such a beastly, inhuman act and call yourself a brahmina! Now I curse you. With all your wounds and fissures, you will have to roam about all over the world for a very long time, stretching almost eternity. Due to the stench that your gaping wounds come close to you, you will have to languish in this hellish state and during this endless course you shall also witness the rule of that boy whom you have just tried to kill in the womb itself." It is believed that Ashwatthama still roams about in this world with his gaping wounds oozing out pus and other obnoxious fluids.

When the time of delivery came, Uttara delivered a dead boy. But Lord Krishna reached there and revived life in that infant. That boy was named Parikshit.

As Parikshit came of age, the Pandavas, having heard of Lord Krishna's quitting his mortal coil, also decided to go to the Himalayas, handing over the kingdom of the earth to Parikshit. The Pandavas also quit their mortal coils along with their common wife, Draupadi, at the Himalayas. There after, Parikshit became the ruler of the Earth.

Though he was an able and kind ruler, his one drawback was his impatient nature. Since he was the scion of the illustrious Pandavas, he faced no opposition from any side and this freedom added to his impatience.

One day he had gone for hunting and went astray on his path, with the result, he lost his way in a dense jungle. All the other members of his retinue were left far behind. While moving aimlessly, he felt thirsty. After much search, he could find a tiny hut and he reached there to get some water. Inside he found an ascetic sitting quietly in meditation. When the king Parikshit, requested him to get him some water, the ascetic remained in his meditation, unconcerned. Parikshit, the king, was not used to having his request go unresponded. Meanwhile, the personified form of Kalyug, sitting ensconced in his crown, added to his arrogance all the more. [This episode will be recounted ahead]. The arrogance further made him impatient and led him to drop a dead snake, lying closeby, round the neck of the mute ascetic.

By that time, his soldiers also reached there, searching for their king and Parikshit returned to Hastinapur. In retrospect he was quite unhappy with himself for having insulted the silent sage so contemptuously. But the arrow had been shot out from the bow.

Meanwhile, that sage-named Shameek kept quiet but his son, Shringi, who was a brilliant sage himself, blew in rage when he heard how his father had been insulted. He was taking a bath with his friends, when this incident took place. At the river itself he got the message that Raja Parikshit had treated his father quite contemptuously. Sorely angry, he said: "These kings of the present age! Not with-standing our king being the scion of great Arjun's family, his conduct is hardly like his high parentage." Then he said to his friends: "Now see the efficiency of my yogic powers. I curse Parikshit that on the seventh day, he would be fatally bitten by the snake-lord, Takshak."

When he reached his hut and spotted the dead snake round his father's neck he once again uttered his curse to Raja Parikshit, hearing which Shameek came out his meditation and said: "Dear son! while you are criticising and cursing Parikshit for his arrogance and impatience, what else are you doing? Don't forget that I provoked the king by not giving him water. I should have been more respectable to him. However, even then, his impetuous anger never deserved the curse you pronounced upon him. He is a kind and able king and the people need such a king, after the massive devastation the humanity has suffered, in the grand war of Mahabharat. Moreover, he is not that type. He must have been misled by some other influence possessing him."

As a matter of fact, Shameek had said the truth though, ignorantly. Raja Parikshit was misled by the evil influence of Kalyug. How Kalyug came in his close contact, happend this way.

After the Mahabharat war was over and Lord Krishna had quitted his mortal coil, the earth felt rather unsafe and shelterless. Assuming the form of a cow, when she was brooding over her bleak future, she happened to meet a bull. That bull was the disguised and personified form of ethical morality or Dharma. Dharma asked Earth as to why she was so forlorn? "Are you being troubled by the rogues. Have the humans started behaving like the beasts?" Earth replied: "You know well Dharma, that in the beginning, in Satyayuga, you stood on your all four legs: Penance, piety, kindness and truth. Then with every subsequent Age you kept on losing your one leg. Now the Age of Kalyug has set in and you, Dharma, stand only on one leg-truth. That too, is being destablished by the evil designs of Kalyug. Now Lord Krishna is back to his eternal realm. Who should I pray for succour now?"

While Earth was talking to Dharma this way, Raja Parikshit happened to overhear their conversation. He immediately spotted Kalyug and challenged him with his sharp-edged sword. That dark form of Kalyug fell at Parikshit's feet, supplicating in a pathitic way: "Where should I reside, O Lord? After all I am a part of the Time Cycle, whose advance no one can stop I can't avoid taking my due turn. You can't kill me either. Since you are the sole emperor of the entire earth, I humbly ask you to show me a place where I could stay to pass my turn on the earth.

"You stay in gambling, drinking intoxicating liquids, womanising and untruthful violence."

"But," Kalyug said: "In my Age these places may be overfull. Tell me another place, King." Thawing with pity on that black existence, Parikshit asked him to stay in gold. As he allowed, Kalyug quickly entered into his crown made of gold. Unknowingly, Parikshit had allowed Kalyug to stay so close to him. It was Kalyug's vile influence, that made Parikshit drop the dead snake round Shameek's neck in arrogance.

Parikshit was, in fact, himself repentant for whatever he had done. Then he heard about Shringa's curse pronounced on him. He decided to do nothing to safeguard himself against that curse. But he wanted to atone for the sin and hear some pious discourse which might improve his soul's lot in the post death domain. He, at once, appointed his son, Janmejaya, as the king and left for the bank of the river Ganga in the company of high sages. There at Shukatala[1], he asked the high sages to recite to him something, which might help him for his wrong doing and at the same time, also improve his soul's lot in the post death-domain.

While the sages were brooding over the sacred text, which would be most opportune for this occasion, there arrived, all of a sudden, 16 year old holy sage, Shukadeva. All rose up to welcome him. After he was duly welcomed, Parikshit asked him: "O Great sage! What should a dying man listen to, to atone for his past deeds and to ensure that his soul's receives a high position, after his body's mortal death? O Sage, I know that I am destined to live not even for 10 more days. Please recite to me something, so that my soul remains engrossed in Lord Krishna's Bhakti (intense devotion)."

Smiling, the adolescent sage Shukadeva replied, "O King! you have asked a very appropriate question. A man about to quit his mortal coil, must concentrate his mind on Lord Krishna, the succour provider to every soul. I think, the best text that ought to be recited at this hour, is the Holy Srimad Bhagwat which my father, sage Vedavyas, created only recently. In fact, I am the only one so far who has heard it. The recitation of this Grand Puran ensures the soul's emancipation and coalescence with that of Super God Krishna."

Then on the request of the assembly of the great sages, Shukadeva Ji recited this Puran for about a week, to the cursed king Parikshit. When the recitation was over, Parikshit was fearless of death and eagerly awaited his soul's coalescence with the supreme spirit.

Those who read this Bhagwat, particularly when death is approaching them, get a high status in Vaikuntha. Since the man doesn't know, when death may approach him, it is better to read or recite this Puran every day, which will cleanse the soul of all kinds of mortal filth.

◻◻

---

1. A picturesque holy spot near modern Muzaffarnagar in U.P. on the bank of the Ganges. It derives its name from Shukadeva.

# 5

# The Description of The Various Incarnations of The Blessed Lord

According to the Srimadbhagwat, there were (one will be) 21 incarnations of the Blessed Lord Vishnu, which are the following:—

**1. SAMAK, SANANDAN, SANATAN AND SANAT-KUMAR:—** The Kaumar Canto says, that these four psychic sons of Brahma were Lord Vishnu's first incarnation. They are described to be very well learned sages but they are perpetually shown as five year old children.

**2. THE 'BOAR' INCARNATION:—** This time Lord Vishnu was incarnated in the form of a 'Boar' or 'Varaha' to retrieve the earth from the ocean's abyss. [In this avtar, he killed Harinyaksha].

**3. THE 'NARAD' INCARNATION :—** The Blessed Lord appeared as the divine sage Narad, who is said to be the psychic son of Brahma. In this avtaar, Narad became a great devotee of Lord Vishnu and is described to be always chanting the name of 'Narayan'. He taught the 'Satvan-Mantra' (the chant to usher in auspiciousness) in this incarnation.

**4. THE 'NARA-NARAYAN' INCARNATION:—** These sages, the inseparable pair of the divine ascetic, were said to have been born by the wife of Dharmaraja, named Moortidevi. In this form, the two ascetics had performed the rigorous penance in Badrikavana (or Badrinath).

**5. THE INCARNATION OF 'KAPIL, THE SAGE':—** In this incarnation, the Blessed Lord created 'Samkhya Shastra,' which he taught to his mother called Devabooti.

**6. THE 'DATTATREYA' INCARNATION:**— He came into the world through the womb of Anosooya, the wife of Sage Atri. Dattatreya, who taught knowledge to various devotees.

**7. THE 'SUYASH' INCARNATION:**— He came to this world through the womb of Aakooti.

**8. THE 'RISHABHADEVA' INCARNATION:**— He was born by Nabiraja's wife Sudevi. In this form, the Blessed Lord displayed the ideal way to those sages, who knew how to discern true knowledge from falsehood, like a 'divine swan,' which knows how to shift pure milk from water. These wise ascetics are, for this reason, called 'Param-Hansa'.

**9. THE INCARNATION AS 'RAJA PRITHU':**— It was on the requests from the high sages, that the Lord condescended to appear as Raja Prithu.

**10. THE 'FISH' INCARNATION:**— When during the Chaakshashu Manvantar the whole world was under the water caused by the big deluge, the Blessed Lord appeared as the 'Great Fish' to guide Vaivasvata Manu's boat to safety.

**11. THE 'TORTOISE' INCARNATION:**— In this incarnation the Blessed Lord appeared in the form of a Tortoise which provided the prop to the mount Mandrachal, when this mount was churned with the help of Vasuki serpent, to bring out gems from the depth of the ocean.

**12. THE 'DHANAVANTRI' INCARNATION:**— In this incarnation, the Blessed Lord appeared as the Divine Vaidya from the ocean, with the pitcher of nectar in his hands, which he gave to the Gods.

**13. THE 'MOHINI' INCARNATION:**— Following the emergence of nectar from the ocean, the demons began to fight against the Gods to have the possession of the nectar pitcher. Then Vishnu, the Blessed Lord, appeared in the form of a very beautiful woman called Mohini (or Enchantress) to dupe the demons and make the Gods imbibe nectar.

**14. THE 'MAN-LION' INCARNATION:**— Appearing as a man with a lionine face, at the request of Prahlad, in this incarnation of 'Narsimha', the blessed Lord tore the demon King Hiranyakashyapa to death.

**15. THE 'DWARF' INCARNATION:—** Appearing as a very short statured brahmin boy, 'Vaman', the Blessed Lord received all the three realms as elms from the demon-King, Bali. He restored Indra to heaven.

**16. THE 'RAM WITH AXE' INCARNATION:—** Appearing as 'Parashuram' the Blessed Lord effaced the existence of the Kashatriyas' becoming increasingly delinquent, as many as 21 times, from the surface of earth.

**17. THE 'VEDAVYAS' INCARNATION:—** In this incarnation the Blessed Lord (Vishnu), properly edited and compiled the different branches of knowledge into four Vedas and Upanishads. And he also created the Fifth Veda, called the Mahabharat.

**18. THE 'RAM' INCARNATION:—** Appearing as the son of Dashrath, the Blessed Lord slayed the demon-lord, Ravana, to rid the earth of all distress.

**19. 'KRISHNA AND BALRAMA' INCARNATIONS:—** As the 20th incarnation, Lord Krishna, the Blessed Lord had appeared with the greatest potency. Balrama was Krishna's elder brother.

**20. THE 'BUDDHA' INCARNATION:—** Appearing as the 'Enlightened one', the Blessed Lord taught the world the lessons in compassion and peace.

**21. THE 'KALKI' INCARNATION:—** This is the only incarnation that is still to take place. The sacred texts claim, that at the end of Kalyug, Kalki Avatar of Lord Vishnu shall take place in the house of a brahmin Vishnuyasha.

*Note:*— Although normally there are only ten incarnations of the Blessed Lord, Vishnu, yet this Purana makes their number become 21. In fact, an incarnation is a mortal person with enough of divine spark, to revive the ascendency of the righteous order and ensure the decline of the demoniac tendencies.

◻◻

# 6

# Brahma Starts The Process of Creation

Before the creation came into existence, the whole world was under the water of the Great Delgue called Pralaya. Lying upon the waves of this water, on his Serpent coil (Shesh-Shaiyya) was Lord Vishnu, lost in his meditative sleep. While he was asleep, there emerged from his navel a beautiful lotus of 14 petals and seated amidst it, was Brahma. He cast a bewildered look all around but couldn't decipher as to where he was. Then he also tried to transverse the stem of the lotus he was born in, but couldn't find its end or begining. At last, he heard a divine voice asking him to start the process of creation without wasting a moment more. "That is the purpose, you have been created for." This was, in fact, the voice of Lord Vishnu. Following the advice, Brahma commenced the process of creation.

He thought of many forms and bodies but he was not satisfied with either of them. At last he hit upon a fully symmetric figure and his first creation were the four boys: Sanaka, Sanatan, Sanata and Sanatkumar who, instead of helping the creator by multiplying themselves, went towards the path of salvation. Though Brahma tried to stop them, they went ahead adamantly on their chosen path. This defiance made Brahma angry, with a frown developing between his eye-brows. It was from that spot that yet another boy was created, who started to cry as soon as he came into existence. Since that boy commenced his life wailing loudly, he came to be known as 'Rudra' [The root 'Rud' in Sanskrit means to wail]. Then after getting the energy from Vishnu, Brahma created his ten psychic sons: Mareechi, Atri, Pulastya, Pulaha, Kratu, Bhrigu, Daksha and Narad. Then Brahma created Goddess Saraswati from his mouth.

But the creator was hardly satisfied having created so many

creatures. He thought of further enhancing his creative world. At that point of time, his body was divided in a twin, with one part emerging as Swayambhoo Manu and the other as a woman called Shataroopa. They were married and their union produced two sons. Priyavrata and Uttanpad and three daughters: Aakooti, Devhooti and Prasooti. Manu solemnised Aakooti's marriage with Ruchi Prajati, Devhooti's with Kardam Sage and that of Prasooti with Daksha Prajapati. It was their progeny that filled the world with human beings.

But since the world was still filled with water–the earth was still beneath it–Manu asked Brahma as to where his progeny should dwell.

Brahma was worried and his worry made a small boar emerge from his nose, which initially was of thumb-nail size. In no time, however, it grew as big as a huge elephant. Brahma was surprised. His progeny as also thinking it to have been caused by the blessed Lord's sportive play (Daivee Leela). While they were still bewildered, that boar became as big as a huge mountain. This spectacle made all hymn to Lord Supreme. Meanwhile, that boar dived into the water and at that time emerged with the earth, resting upon its nose thorn. Then the earth was established at its proper position above water. Since then, the earth stays above water. Having redeemed the earth, that boar vanished.

It has been already mentioned, Goddess Saraswati was Brahma's creation. Seeing his daughter, so beautiful and wise, Brahma developed enormous feelings for her. He rushed to her to satisfy his peaking libido. Seeing him commiting this most prohibitive sin, his psychic sons Mareechi and Atri prevented him from doing so. They admonished their Sire: "What sin are you going to commit? What will happen to your entire creation if its Creator commits such heinous acts. You should, instead, set precedents for it, to follow so that it may remain auspicious. Don't do such lowly acts, O Sire!"

Brahma realised his mistake. He was quite remorseful. At that very moment he quitted his form. It is claimed that, Brahma's quitted body was dissolved in the space and now occasionally shows itself in the form of fog and darkness.

However, owing to his yogic powers, he could get another, more brilliant body. He again started the process of creation with greater composure. This time, he created the Vedas from his mouth. Even then, the process of creation could not gain the desired chain of the process. He again, grew frustrated and again divided his body in two parts which became Manu and Shatroopa again. It was this union, which can be said to be the origin of the creation, created out of copulation between the male and female entities of the chosen species. Hence this creation came to be known as 'Maithuni Srishtai'. [Maithun in Sanskrit means copulation]. Thus, the process of creation assumed self sufficiency.

❐❐

# 7

# Sage Kardem Helps in The Process of Creation

As mentioned earlier, Brahma created the world assuming a variety of forms. He created the Daityas, Danava, Gandharva, Kinnar, Apsaras, the Pitiriganas etc. in his different forms. But there were many obstructions in the process. Once he shook his body in frustration, so violently as to make his body bristles shed off, which originated the species of snake called 'ahi'.

However, it was from Manu and Shataroopa that his creation could get a sembalance of the autocreative process through male and female's physical union. It is from Manu that the term 'manava' (which means man in Sanskrit) has been derived.

Manu's daughter Devahooti was married to sage Kardam. He had performed rigorous penance for 10,000 years on the bank of the river Saraswati. Lord Vishnu, then appeared before him and granted him the desired boon of marriage: "You will get the offer from the daughter of Manu and Shatroopa, who will themselves come to you with the offer. From this union, you will not get only nine daughters but I will also incarnate into the world through your wife's womb.

As ordained, one day sage Kardam was sitting in his hermitage when Manu and Shataroopa gave him the offer. The sage agreed to marry Devahooti. He married off his nine daughters in the following way. His daughter called Kala was given in marriage to Mareechi, Ansooya to Atri, Shraddha to Angira and Havirbhoo to Pulasya. Pulaha received Gati, Kriya to Kritu, Khyati to Bhrigu, Arundhati to Vashishtha and Shanti to Atharva sage.

Then, in order to fulfil his commitment, Vishnu appeared as Kapil–a son to Kardam and Devahooti.

Since, Kardam knew about Shri Hari (Vishnu's) this incarnation, he privately prayed to Lord: "O Lord! You are omniscient and know every secret of your devotee's heart. I know you have come into the world for granting the Sankhya-knowledge."

Where upon Shri Hari (Kapil) said "O sage! This rare knowledge leading to self-realisation, was growing increasingly extinct. It is to re-enlighten the world with this knowledge that I assumed this form. Now I release you from all familial bondage. You may depart for meditation, as I will impart this knowledge first to my mother. On learning this, she will also be freed from mortal bonds."

Kardam Sage was delighted to get his cherished freedom. He reverntally circumambulated around Kapil (his son as the incarnation of Lord Krishna) and left happily towards jungle. Soon through his meditation, he started viewing every one as the manifestation of one Supreme spirit and this vision made his soul attain the highest realm of beautitude.

After his father's departure, Kapil started living in the 'Bindusar Teertha' along with his mother.

One day his mother requested him: "O My son, the Incarnation of the Blessed Lord! please also make me enlightened by granting me the Sankhya knowledge, showing the way to Self-Realisation".

Then Kapil lectured her on this rare knowledge, whose essence was "God is the only true entity and the rest of the world is unreal." This self-realisation opens one's inner eyes to this true wisdom.

Giving her this supreme knowledge, Kapil also left for the woods as his mother's soul was also emancipated.

◻◻

# 8

# The Progeny of Manu's Daughters

Manu's daughter Aakooti was married to Ruchi Prajapati under the condition of the 'Putrika Marriage', which specified that the first son of the daughter would be given back to the daughter's father. Manu's third daughter Prasooti was married to Daksha Prajapati. Thus the five issues of Manu, his two sons: Priyavrata and Uttanapad and his three daughters mentioned above can be held to be the origin of all creation. The sage Kardam's one daughter Kala had given birth to the son called Poornam, who also had one daughter Kala and one son. The name of the daughter was Devakulya, who was reborn in the next life as the river Ganga. That Sage Atri and Anusooya had son called Dattatreya, had already been mentioned. How he was born, is explained below.

When Brahma asked sage Atri to enhance creation he first worshipped Lord Hari (Vishnu) who made all the three Super deities: Brahma, Vishnu, Mahesh appear before the sage Atri and Anusooya. The sage requested them to be born in his house, with their essential spirits personified. The three deities said: "Be it so" and they departed. At due time, Lord Vishnu appeared as the couple's son Dattatrey, Shiva as the second son, Durvasa (renowned for his deadly temper) and Brahma appeared as their third son Chandrama (or the Moon).

Manu's third daughter Prasooti, as mentioned before, was married to Daksha Prajapati. Their union produced sixteen daughters. Out of them, thirteen were married to Dharma (the death God), One to Agni (Fire-God) and one to the Prithvigana (the category of manas). Another daughter with the name Shakti was married to Lord Shiva but she immolated herself to death before she could beget any issue. She did so, detecting a ranked insult shown by her father in a Yagya ceremony in which no oblation was offered to Shiva.

❏❏

# 9

# Daksha's Hostility for Shiva And Sati's Death By Self-Immolation

Once in a Yagya, when Prajapati Daksha reached the venue, all the rishis (Sages) and seers (Muni's) as also the Gods rose up to welcome him except Shiva and Brahma. While Daksha didn't take offence at the indifference shown to him by Brahma, owing to the latter being his father, he was greatly offended at Shiva's contempt. After all, Shiva was his son-in-law, being married to his daughter called Sati or Shakti.

Daksha couldn't check his anger and blurted out. "It was my mistake to have given my daughter in marriage to this ill-clad and ash-smearing Shiva, addicted to narcotic drugs. He is no good. Since I am the senior Prajapati, I order that hence forth, no oblation should be offered to Shiva in any Yagya."

Shiva's one favourite henchman, Nandi was very much there and he blew up. "Those who are hostile to Shiva are the animals and Daksha is one. Let him be the one with a goat face, which keeps on speaking only one word. I....I (Main-Main). Such arrogant persons deserve that face. And all those who support him can't either escape their devastation one day."

Bhrigu, the sage, who was also there, found Nandi to be over reacting in anger. When he tried to check him, Nandi grew all the more angry and said: "Keep quite you hater of Shiva. Soon you will learn manners." This hurt Bhrigu and he countered by pronouncing the following curse: "Shiva's all henchmen and devotees, shall always be mostly fradulent addicted to various drugs."

Meanwhile, listening to this kind of lowly and cheap words, Shiva felt disgusted and he left for Kailash.

It was following many months that Shakti found scores of chariots and palanquin's and planes (vimanas) leaving for kailash. When she asked one passer by, he replied: "Having been appointed the head of the Dakshas, Daksha has announced to hold a masive Yagya to celebrate the occasion."

Sati was hurt to know that her father had neglected her as well as his son-in-law, the renowned Mahadeva. She thought that they must also go to protest against it and broached the topic before her husband. Shiva said: "Of course there is no harm in going to one's father's house uninvited but going there on a special occasion is against the norm of propriety in my view. Perhaps his hostility to me, also made him neglect you."

But Sati was adamant. She said: "He carries the hostility and not us. We have an open heart. Let me know, what is the basic reason behind this imprudence on the part of my father."

Though Shiva tried to deter her, she would not listen. At last Shiva instructed his henchpersons to escort Sati to her father's place.

When she reached there, she was aghast. None-except her mother welcomed her. Her father had even tried to question her arrival, without any invitation. But when she reached the holy canopy of the Yagya, she was really angry. No part of the oblation was assigned to Shiva. She was deeply hurt; "How could my father be so impudent? Does he think his personal hostility to Shiva can be more than Grand God's status? My Lord is one of the three primary Agents to accomplish the Supreme Spirit's will."

At once, she decided to end her life as Daksh's daughter. She couldn't tolerate any relation with the hater of Shiva. Immediately she created a 'Yagya-Fire' from her body and burnt herself to death.

When the henchpersons of Shiva, who had reached there escorting Sati, saw Sati's fiery end, they created a havoc in the venue. They destroyed the yagya, as much as they could, and rushed to Shiva to inform him about his wife's suicide. Shankar was livid in rage hearing the news. In anger, he plucked out a hair from his head and threw it at a stone slab. As the hair hit the slab, there appeared an eerie, huge bodied three eyed-figure. That was a part of Shiva's devastation for Rudra and was called 'Veerabhadra'. Shiva ordered him to devastate the Yagya and teach his caluminators a fitting lesson.

Veerabhadra reached the venue with a batallion of Shiva's henchmen. So far only inanimate bodies of that yagya were destroyed, now the henchmen began to harass the seers and sages present there. Seeing them, sage Bhrigu chanted a deadly Mantra to produce an army of Gods called 'Ribhus', each carrying a live torch to take on the henchmen of Shiva. But in no time, Daksha was slayed, with his head hacked off by Veerabhadra with a sharp axe. They tore away most of the beard on Bhrigu's face. Then setting the whole venue on fire, they all tracked back to Kailash.

Meanwhile, the severely beaten, Gods rushed to Brahma's shelter. But Brahma cluded all the Gods and sages for showing a wilful neglect to Shiva. "How could you all dare insult the Jagadeesh? His henchpersons taught you the right lesson. Now if you want that Yagya to be completed, go back to Shiva and seek his forgiveness."

When the Gods and sages did so, Shiva told them: "It is Daksha's arrogance that cost him his life. But I'm pleased with you all and promise to accept the oblation again. I'd have things restored back to normalcy."

Although Bhrigu's beard was restored, and Posha's teeth were repaired, the question arose as to, how to revive Daksha, whose head had been consumed by the holy fire. At last, Nandi's curse on Daksha became true and a goat's head was implanted on his head. Life was revived in his body and as soon as he became conscious, he sought forgiveness from Shiva, who readily obliged.

◻◻

# 10

## The Sun's Transitional Phase and Speed of Movement

The Sun transits every Zodiac sign in a period of one month. The zodiac signs are: Aries, Taurus, Gemini, Cancer, Leo, Virgo, Libra, Scorpio, Sagitarius, Capricorn, Aquarious and Pisces. In the first five signs the solar speed gets reduced by a Ghadi (nearly 24 minutes). That is the reason, why winters have shortened days and long nights. The trend gets reversed in the other signs and we have more of sun light. The sun becomes north-going (Uttarayana), when it transits into the Capricorn sign and becomes south-going when it reaches the Gemini sign. During its south-ward slant, the days become longer and the night shorter.

The orbit of the Sun, according to Shrimadbhagwat, is 9 crore 51 lakh Yojan around Manasottar mountain and the sun keeps revolving around the Sumeru mount. The dwellers of this mount, experience the sun always at its zenith.

The Srimadbhagwat claims, that like the sun all the other planets and satellites also remain on the move perpetually, orbiting the sun. It says that in one "Muhurta" the chariot of the sun covers 34 lakh 800 yojan which is belived to be the perimeter of the chariot's wheel. This wheel is called 'Samvatasara', which has 12 spokes, each defining one of the six seasons and three naves (Anawan), which define four quarters (Four months group).

The capacity of the chariot stretches to 36 lakh Yojan in length and 9 lakh yojan in width. Its charioteer is called Aruna and seven horses are yoked in this chariot to pull this chariot ahead. This Sun-

God covers 2000 yojan distance in every fraction of a second and goes round the full zodiac, stretching to 9 crore 51 lakh yojan, staying in one zodiac sign for one month. Each season comprises two months and each month has two fortnights. The bright one is called 'Shukla-Paksha' and the dark one is called 'Krishna-Paksha'.

❑❑

# 11

## The Tale of Priyavrata

Swayambhoo Manu, as already mentioned, had two sons: Priyavrata and Uttanapad. The eldest son of Uttanpada was Dhruva who was a well known figure. He had pleased Lord Hari at a very young age (he was only five years old then) to get his immovable position in the sky, even now the pole Star is called Dhruva Tara[1].

Manu's eldest son Priyavrata was a self-realised person. He, having received the supreme knowledge from sage Narad, became quite indifferent to entering family life. Meanwhile, the worry of the Grandsire Brahma was that his creation must multiply. When Priyavrata refused to listen to his father, Manu's order, Brahma himself reached him to instruct: "Since you are already initiated in the worship of Lord Hari, you are a self-realised soul. But remember, this whole creation survives on the inkling received from Lord Hari. No one can defy his order. And it is He, who wants the creation to multiply, so you must enter family life and enjoy all pleasures. When the due time comes, you shall automatically grow averse to all such sunsual delights. But in the mean time, you can't defy the order of Lord Hari."

At last, Priyavrata heeded to this advice. He was married to Prajapati Vishwakarma's daughter, Bahirshmati. Then entrusting all duties of the state to Priyavrata, Manu retired to the jungles. Raja Priyavrata ruled for many thousands years. He had ten sons and one daughter who was married to Shukracharya, the Demon-Guru.

One day he took the resolve of eliminating darkness from his kingdom. Sitting in a bright chariot drawn by the steeds, as fast as

---

1. The story of Dhruva has been given in details in the Vishnu Purana of the same series of books. Only brief reference, therefore, is being given.

that of the Sun, he circumambulated seven times around the earth. The Srimad Bhagwat claims, that the grooves caused by his chariot-wheels movement, subsequently became the seven seas, which also divided the earth into seven continents. He gave his seven sons those continents to rule, one to each. But his there sons grew averse to worldly duties and retired to jungles to meditate and realise God. This made Priyavrata also, long for the life devoid of worldly bounds. He, at once, went to Narad and said: "Enough is enough, O Divine Sage! Now show me the path that may provide salvation to my soul." And when Narad instructed him, leaving his wife to manage the worldly affair, Priyavrata, finally left to worship Lord Hari.

Seeing his father quitting the world for pursuing his meditation, his one son, named Aagneedhra began to look after the Kingdom and people. Once he happened to reach a picturesque valley of Mandrachal and devoted himself to penance for self-realisation. This made Brahma again worried. He sent a beautiful Apsara, called Poorvachitti from his realm to seduce the son of Priyavrata and make him return to the normal world. That beautiful danseuse from Brahma's realm cast her charms upon Aagneedhara so overwhelmingly, that he stopped his meditation and followed the woman in captivating love. Then he enjoyed all sensual bliss in the company of Poorvachitti and produced nine sons. For many years he ruled the Kingdom and enjoyed the mortal pleasures.

□□

# 12

# The Tale of Raja Prithu

It was in devotee Dhruva's family, where Raja Prithu was born. Although his father Vena was a tyrant dictator, who tortured noble men and brahminas alike, Prithu himself was a very noble king. He is also believed to be a partial incarnation of Vishnu. When Prithu was installed as the king of the earth, the people were in a severely distressed condition. The earth was devoid of adequate food and hence majority of the people were starving. One sage told Prithu, that the earth had deliberately hidden all its edibles, cereals etc. inside its interior. This made the noble king Prithu furious and he took out his bow and arrows to threaten the earth. When the earth found no one capable of coming to her rescue, she surrendered and on coming to Raja Prithu's shelter, asked: "Were you planning to keep the creation on water, when I would be destroyed?"

The King replied: "No doubt it would have been difficult but one who treats the beings of my kingdom so callously, needs to be punished. I know it is sacrilege to cast weapons on a lady but you almost forced me to do so. Why have you hidden all the eatables inside your womb?"

The earth apologised, saying that she did so out of fear of the tyrants ruling the earth. Then she added handbound: "Now you are my king and you have the liberty to exploit my bounty to the hilt. But you must arrange for a calf to make me offer you everything liberally and you must also arrange for a fitting pot to put all the largesse that I would offer to you. It was to protect my resources from being looted by the rogues, that I hid them deep inside me. Now it is up to you, as to how to extract that natural treasure from my womb."

Raja Prithu was satisfied. He immediately asked Manu to act as a calf and with his own hand he made the cow-like earth offer all the natural bounty. Then he asked Gods and the high sages to act as the calf, to receive the gifts from the earth[1]. Raja Prithu was delighted to receive the gifts from the earth. Hence one of the earth's epithet is Prithu, which means 'of Prithu.' [The moral enshrined is that he, who treats the earth like Raja Prithu did, she offers all her bounties liberally].

Raja Prithu conducted more than a 100 Ashwamedha Yagya, having received all the natural wealth and over lordship of the entire earth. He performed the Yagyas so famously that even the Lord Hari, accompanied by all Gods, attended them to personally accept the offered oblations.

However, on seeing Prithu's unprecedented prosperity, Indra developed jealousy for him. He was apprehensive, lest the king should capture his divine kingdom as well. With the result, blinded by jealousy, Indra quietly managed to steal the consecrated horse of the 100th Yagya. But when Indra was clandestinely going heavenwards with the stolen horse, sage Atri saw him. He reported the matter to King Prithu, who ordered his son to catch hold of Indra. Indra was in a disguise. He had adopted the form of a brahmina ascetic with his whole body smeared with ash. So, even when he reached near Indra, deeming him to be a holy ascetic, the son of Prithu returned empty handed. But sage Atri told him: "That is Indra and no one else." Then Prithu's son was again sent to nab the culprit. Seeing him coming close behind, Indra disappeared, leaving the horse. The son of Prithu merrily caught hold of that horse and returned to the venue of the Yagya. It was kept there tied to a peg. But seizing his opportunity, Indra again managed to steal away that horse. When the sage Atri noticed the theft, he again asked the son of Prithu to go to capture Indra. But as soon as the Prithu Kumar (son of Prithu) set his arrow

---

1. **It is an allgorical way of saying that Manu's seers, sage and gods properly exploiteed the natural bounty which was subsequently arranged by Raja Prithu.**

on the bow to aim it at Indra, the divine Lord quickly fled, leaving the horse again. When Prithu learnt about Indra's conspiracy, he was furious. But he was pacified by the high sages. They told him: "Since you are performing the Yagya, you can't kill anybody. Save the consecrated animal. But don't worry", they assured, "We will chant such mantras which may force Indra to be drawn into the holy fire pit." Saying so, the holy sages invoked Indra. As they were about to offer the special oblation to the holy fire to cause Indra's immolation, there appeared Brahma. He advised Prithu: "You and Indra, both, are the partial incarnations of the Blessed Lord. Moreover, since your aim is salvation of the soul, why must you perform these Yagyas? Don't worry for the completion of your 100th Yagya. Stop the ceremony now. First you must destroy the inequity that is being done, out of Indra's jealousy."

As he was about to follow Brahma's instructions, there also appeared the Blessed Lord Vishnu with Indra in tow. The Lord said, "I am happy with you. Now you also forgive Indra, who tried to disturb your Yagya. The bounden duty of a king is to protect his people. You are supremely wise and the wise-realised souls see their enemy also as a friend. You are my great devotee. You may have any desired boon from me." Raja Prithu was more than gratified, to have the blessed Lord before him. Meanwhile, Indra fell flat at the king's feet to seek his forgiveness. Prithu quickly raised him up and pressed him to his heart.

Then Raja Prithu said: "O Blessed Lord! I want no boon to enjoy these mortal pleasures. If you really want to bless me with a boon, then make me listen to your glories for a thousand years. Nothing, except this, is my wish."

The Blessed Lord blessed him and said: "Your steadfast devotion to me has virtually won me over. You shall get all you want. Now righteously rule the state and look after your people."

As the Blessed Lord was about to depart, Raja Prithu washed his feet and put that water upon his head. The blessed Lord Hari vanished, thereafter.

When Raja Prithu became old enough, he appointed his son as

the king and retired to the jungles with his wife Archi. There the couple began to perform a very severe penance and, at last, keeping his mind fixed to the memory of the Blessed Lord, Prithu quitted his mortal coil. His wife also ended her life on the pyre of her dead husband. Soon a Vimana (divine aerial vehicle) reached there to take the king and his wife's souls to the realm of the Blessed Lord, Vaikuntha.

□□

# 13

## Ajaamil's Salvation

Many eras ago, there lived a brahmina in the city of Kannauj (Kanya-kubja). His name was Ajaamil. Although he was a very honest and religious minded person, once he happened to see a Shoodra enjoying the company of a prostitute. He was so much titillated by the spectacle, that he ceased to follow the righteous path. He also sought the company of a nautch-girl. Their association inculcated many vices and bad habits in him. He started drinking wine and gambling. He had ten sons. The name of the youngest son was 'Narayana' who was his father's pet. When the prostitutes duped him and fled with all the gold that Ajaamil had, he had become quite old. Resignedly he came back to his family and soon his death approached.

Ajaamil was nervous, feeling his heart sinking. In panic he started calling his pet son, "Narayana...Narayana!" As he pronounced 'Narayan'. (one of the epithet of the Blessed Lord Hari), the approaching messengers of death were immediately obstructed by the messengers of Lord Hari. The death messengers were taken aback. "How come your lord has sent you all, to protect the life of this ranked sinner.. He had been a filthy being, indulging in all sorts of vices and commiting all possible sins. He doesn't deserve to be protected by you."

The messengers of Lord Vishnu replied: "Well, sin and vices are comparative terms. Even then, the moment he chanted 'Narayana', it became our Lord's duty to protect him."

"But that is his son's name. He yelled for his son 'Narayana' and not your Lord", the death messengers told Vishnu's messengers.

"No matter how one chants or with what intention, if one chants our Lord's name, he immediately comes under his protection. Since he has chanted the name of 'Narayana' many a times, that holy sound has washed away his sins. Hence we won't let you grab his soul and take him to your realm."

The death messengers felt helpless before the henchmen of Lord Hari. Ajaamil's life was saved, but Ajaamil could overhear the conversation between the death messengers and henchmen of Lord Vishnu. He quietly bowed his head to Lord Vishnu and then he left for Haridwar to atone for the sins he had commited. His inner eye were now open. He realised how he had been wasting his life with his indulgence in vices and all ethernal worldly pursuits. He developed real devotion for Vishnu, after his escape from death by a hair's breadth. And this time, when he finally died he found not the death-messenger but the messenger of Vishnu approaching him. The mere chant of 'Narayana-Narayana' had not only given a fresh lease of life but also improved his post-death status. Now his soul was escorted to Vaikunth, the ultimate abode.

◻◻

# 14

# Rishabha Deva and Jada-Bharat

King Aagneedhra, the son of Priyavrata, had a son called Nabhi. Though he was a very powerful and noble king, he had no male issue. So he asked the sages to perform a Yagya, which might ensure him a son. That they did and propitiated the presiding deity of the Yagya, who appeared in person. Seeing the sages worshipping God to bless the king with a son, the Lord granted the desired boon. Then the sages said: "Please bless us also with an unwavering devotion to you. Hence we request such a son to our king, who may be an exact copy of youself." Where upon, the presiding deity, who was Lord Hari himself, replied with a smile, "You have asked me to give an impossible boon. I am unique as I don't have any one like me. But, in order to make your wish fulfilled, I may myself appear as Nabhi's son."

At due time, Lord Hari incarnated at Nabhi's house. The king called him Rishabha. He was a precocious child and soon mastered all knowledge. Once it didn't rain in that kingdom for many years. Then Rishabha used his yogic powers to make the clouds rain. The people were delighted, and bowing to their wish, Raja Nabhi appointed Rishabha Deva as the king. Even Indra was pleased with him and gave him his daughter Jayanti, in marriage. This union, produced a hundred sons to Rishabha Deva. The eldest among them was Bharat. It is after his name, that this part of the world came to be called Bharat-Varsha[1]. He always worked for people's welfare.

Once while roaming about the various realms, he reached

---

1. Some ancient accounts claim that it was not this Bharat but Bharat, the son of Dushyant and Shakuntala, that made our land called Bharatvarsha.

Brahma's realm. And seeking blessings from Brahma, returned to teach his sons the following way, "As soon as the soul acquires this human body, it makes the body infatuated with sensual cravings. Whereas, the man should always treat this rare body as the stepping stone to aquire higher status for the soul. One should never be bound by the ego-sense. The wise, who know this secret must guide the mislead people."

After making everyone happy, he appointed Bharata as the king and departed to the jungles to meditate. But Bharat was totally averse to all the worldly bounds. However he too happened to develop a great love for a deer-ling[1], which made him lose, his this life. His story tells us, that any infatuation for the worldly bounds can cause one's downfall, no matter how wise-that person be. Bharat, called Jadabharata for his insensitivity to his body needs, was reborn in human species again and whose worshipping God, he finally quit his mortal coil to make his body coalesce with the supreme spirit.

□□

---

1. The detailed story is given in **Vishnu Purana** of the same series.

# 15

## The Dwarf (Vamana) Incarnation

Once troubled by the demons, Gods were greatly distressed, passing their days while hiding themselves in the deep caves of the Himalayas. The Gods' mother, Aditi, was quite worried. She asked her husband, sage Kashyapa as to what should be done to provide relief to her sons. Kashyapa said, "Only one can provide relief to them, Lord Hari. Since you are their mother, you must worship him only. Continue-this fast for 12 days surviving on only milk. Conclude the fast after feeding 'Kheer' to the noble brahmins. May be, this penance brings the desired result."

Aditi perfomred the penance with full devotion. Propitiated, the Lord Hari appeared before her and said: "I know what you want. But at present your sons' welfare can't be assured. However, I promise that soon I shall come to the world through your womb, to rid them of their all troubles."

At due time Aditi got pregnant. Her family way filled Kashyapa's hermitage with a divine light. At the appointed time, she delivered a son, who was rather dwarfish in stature. This earned the new-born an epithet 'Vamana''. At the time of his sacred thread ceremony, Brihaspati gave him the thread, the Earth, the lion-skin to cover his private parts, the Moon gave the royal staff, Brahma his Kamandala, the Sky the canopy, the Seven Seers the Kushgrass matt, Goddess Saraswati the Rudraksha beeds' garland, father Kashyapa the waist chain and mother the strip, to tie his waist with.

---

1. It is mentioned that Vaman earned this epithet because his total height was 52 fingers breadth put together.

At that time, the demon lord was Bali. In order to perform his 100th Ashwamedh Yagya, the demon King had chosen a huge spot on the bank of river Narmada. For ensuring the Gods' welfare, Vamana reached the venue of the Yagya. Since the Gods had no territory in their control, they had no option but to remain hiding in the caves. Seeing Vamana approaching there, spreading brilliance all around, the brahmin priests thought, as though Lord Sun was coming there to bless the king himself. But Shukracharya thought, as though the child sage Sanata Kumar or the Fire-God himself was reaching the venue. All rose up to give Vaman a most thunderous welcome. The king said, "I welcome you, O celebrated child sage. What should I do to please you."

Vamana said: "O King! You belong to a very noble family. Your grand father, Prahlad's devotion to Lord Hari is renowned in all the three realms. I learnt that you have inherited some of those traits from your grand father. I only want a piece of land to stay over, as you own three realms. This is my meagre request."

The king felt reassured listening to this meagre wish of the child-like brahmin. He had an apprehension, confirmed by his Guru Shukracharya, that the arrival of Vamana could be a part of the God's conspiracy. King Bali knew, that going by his own renown, he couldn't have refused the gift of all the three realms to Vamana. Hence, he felt quite happy to listen to his trifling demand.

He said, rather complacently, "How much land do you need, brahmin?"

Vamana said, "As much as my three steps could measure." Bali quite happily allowed him to have this much of land. As he did so, Vamana's size began to grow enormously and soon his head was lost in the clouds. Although Shukracharya tried to deter Bali from giving such a boon, as he had detected Lord Hari's presence in Vamana, the king refused to eat back his words. Infuriated, the demon Guru cursed his king, "You will become devoid of all wealth. Yet undaunted, Raja Bali did maintain his commitment. Meanwhile, Vamana had been growing all this period. Since King Bali had already donated that part of the land which the dwarf Brahman's three steps could cover, he kept on quietly watching the dwarf becoming a giant of unheard proportions.

Having attained his desired stature, the dwarf began to measure the land. In the first step he measured the entire earth and in the second the heaven, leaving no place which he could measure by his third step. It is said that in this process, when he put his second step covering heaven, Brahma reventially washed that foot with his Kamandal water. It is this water, which is the origin of the river Ganga which flowed in heavens and much later, at the request of Bhagirath and his ancestors, condescended to come down on to the earth. Hence Ganga's one of the epithets is 'Vishnupadi' i.e. originating from the feet of Lord Vishnu.

Seeing the Lord duping them, the demons got angry and started attacking Gods. But they were restrained by their King Bali who said, "Don't fight! Thus far we were enjoying our waxing glory, now it is the Gods' turn. But you all must feel elated, that the Supreme God Vishnu had to come to your King in the form of a beggar." The demons checked themselves and retired to the Patal-lok (nether world) to pass their time, lying low.

Than Vamana accosted Bali, "King! You had promised me to give the land which my three steps could measure. Now there is no place, which my third step can cover. You must show me the place or else you shall be eating your words."

Raja Bali said with a bowed head, "Bhagwan! I'm not going back on my words. You can place your third step over my head." And saying so, he bowed his head all the more. The Lord, pleased with the demon king's conduct praised him, "You are truly a grandson of your grandfather. You shall be renowned as the most veridicious demon king." And saying so, having accomplished the objective of providing succour to the Gods, Lord Vishnu decided to return to his realm, Vaikuntha. But before he could do so, there arrived Prahlad, the grandfather of Bali. Since Bali had failed to fulfill his total commitment, Garuda, the mount of Lord Hari, bound him in his famous noose called the Garuda Pash.

The crown jewel of the devotees, Prahlad, first hymned the glories of his chosen Lord Vishnu and then said: "Lord! You give and take away gifts to your devotees in a bizzare, yet, captivating manner. You are unique, Lord!"

At that time, Raja Bali's wife also reached there. After reverentially bowing to Vamana, she said, "O Lord! He had committed no fault, as he had given whatever he had, including his own body. Now he shouldn't be penalised. He ought to be released from the deadly 'Garuda Pash'."

Brahma, reaching there, also requested for the release of Bali. Then Bhagwan Vamana said, "Raja Bali remained firm on his dharma (the bounded duty). Hence he can't be punished. Now he shall be Indra in the seventh Manavatar (Era of Manu). Meanwhile, he will dwell in Sutala, a distinct realm to be created by Vishwakarma." Then addressing Bali, Lord Hari said: "I grant you the boon of eternal welfare. You should go to Sutala realm to dwell there till the 7th Manavavtara. I shall stay there as the sentinel of the realm, to safeguard your security."

Raja Bali was overwhelmed with emotion and gratitude. "I got something which the great sages receive after ions of their penance." At that very moment the 'Garuda Pash' released him automatically. Bali fell flat before Lord Hari (Vamana). Then with his entire family, he departed to Sutala Lok.

Then Lord Hari gifted heaven again to Indra. Prahlad was still there. Lord Hari advised him: "Go and dwell with your grandson, Bali. There you will be able to have my frequent Darshana." As they went, then came Shukracharya who said: "Lord! Now who should complete the Yagya left incomplete? The King is gone."

Lord Hari said: "You should complete this Yagya, left incompleted by King Bali. Nevertheless, he would get full credit for it."

Thus Vamana (Lord Hari, Vishnu) gifted the three realms' rulership back to his elder brother Indra. Subsequently Vamana also came to be known as Upendra.

◻◻

# 16

## Shiva Falls for Mohini

After the great churning of the Ocean[1], when the pitcher of nectar emerged, the Gods and demons were engaged in a fierce fight to drink nectar. This created a trouble, which Brahma could think no solution of. At last, he and Shiva approached Lord Hari and he asked them to wait, as he would soon find a trick to calm down the situation. And in no time, there appeared a very comely woman mesmerising all. She was called Mohini, who was Lord Vishnu in disguise. She (Mohini) appeared particularly enchanting to the demons, whose attention, she captured instantly. They left the nectar and ran after the woman. She said to the demons, "Don't fight over this nectar. Let me distribute it to you all. But since the sensity of nectar is greater at the bottom, I advise you all to let the Gods drink first the upper part, which is in fact quite diluted. Let me be through with them and then I will let you drink the real essence of nectar."

Captivated by her charms already, the demons agreed to her suggestion and Vishnu in the form of Mohini began to pour nectar down the Gods' throat without any problem. However there was a demon called Viprachitti who saw-through the 'Mohini's' game. Realising that after the Gods' turn, nothing would be left for the demons to imbibe, he quietly slipped into the Gods' queue for drinking nectar. But the Moon-God and the Sun-God recognised the demon in his disguise. By that time nectar had reached upto the demon's throat. As Vishnu cast his disc Sudarshana, the demon's throat was slit with the head falling down, but owing to the effect of nectar, the demon

---

1. This event has been described at length in Shiva Purana of this series of books.

was still alive. His head and trunk became, separate living entities. They are now called Rahu and Ketu, respectively. That is why, it is believed mythologically, that at the time of solar eclipse, the trunk part or Ketu covers Sun while in the case of Lunar eclipse, Rahu covers the Moon. This way, they keep on taking the revenge on the luminaries (the Sun and the Moon) for revealing their identity.

Many years later, Lord Shiva, while sitting in his abode at Kailash Mount, was reminded of this incident, when Vishnu adopted the form of an 'enchantress'. He wanted to impress upon his wife Sati, as to how much beautiful a woman could be. Then he said: "Let us go to Lord Hari's realm and request the Lord to readopt that form and show it to you."

"O, Lord" said Mahadeva, perhaps high on his favourite narcotic 'Bhang' [cannabis indica]. "What brouht me here, is the longing to see you again in that most captivating Mohini form. Would you do it again for me?"

Smiling, the Lord, whose 'maya' deludes even the most learned and wise, said: "Very well! But that time I adopted that form with a definite purpose. I wanted to deprive the vile demons from drinking nectar. But now you want me to put up that show for your pleasure. I don't mind it but you have to be particularly careful just in case the woman's beauty enchants you totally." Lord Vishnu said in a light banter and disappeared. Shiva and Sati were left there, waiting for the 'Show'. Soon they found a most pleasant atmosphere appearing before them. Cool, fragrance-laden breeze was flowing, birds were chirping and flowers were blooming. And there appeared, beneath a mango tree a most beautiful woman, wearing very seductive clothes, which were more revealing than concealing her velvety contours. She had a rubber ball in her hand, which she was throwing at the ground and prancing with it, making her sensuous body all the more titillating. Shiva was over whelmed with her charms and was, unmindfully, sexually aroused. Forgetting everything else, he started running madly after that woman. Seeing him trailing her, she started to run even faster, making her body even more captivating to the eyes, as her body appeared more exposed. Running madly after her, at last Shiva was able to catch her in a close embrace. As he ejaculated, he suddenly became concious, of his state. Immediately he stopped, feeling terribly embarrased. The Srimad Bhagwat claims, that the mines of gold, silver and lime were created, where his ejaculated semen fell.

But Lord Hari realised his embarrassment. He said to Lord Shankar, coming in his original form, "Don't feel embarrassed as this is the effect of my Maya. It is only you, who could come out of its effect on your own. Now I bless you that henceforth you will never be affected from my Maya."

Having seen the form of Mohini, both Lord Shiva and his spouse returned to Kailash, singing the glories of the Lord Hari.

◻◻

# 17

## Lord Hari Saves The Elephant, Gajendra Moksha

It is a very popular tale for the devotees of Lord Vishnu, which shows the Super God takes care of everybody. Called the 'Gajendra Moksha'[1] this is a popular tale among the Vaishnavites.

Many eras ago, there was a huge mount called Trikoota in the Ocean of milk[2]. Its three peaks were marked by silver, iron and gold coatings, which used to radiate, as much shine as, to make the area lighted always. Nearby was also a very beautiful forest, always echoing with the sweet chirping sounds cooed by a score of birds. Not far from it was also a beautiful pond, renowned for its ambrosial water. That was the spot, where a King elephant used to come to bathe with its queens. It was a massive elephant and as powerful to shoo even the deadly beasts away, by its mere presence. It was massive and very heavy. Once it was taking his merry bath in that pond, when a huge crocodile clutched at his foot. Now the elephant was in real trouble. No doubt he tried to wriggle himself out of that pond, but due to his own heavy weight he couldn't do so. Then he cried in utter distress for he had exhausted all his power. His own weight was adding to his problem. So, finding no relief he made a prayer to the Lord Hari [This prayer, as already mentioned, is called Gajendra moksha.

---

1. The translation of this prayer is given at the end of this story.
2. There is much difference in the various accounts available about the actual place where the elephant was trapped by a crocodile. Some say it happened in the ocean while some claim its happening at the confluence of the Ganga and Sonebhadra rivers.

It has been called from the 8th canto of the Srimad Bhagwat.

The narrator of this Srimad Bhagwat, Sage Shukadeva, recites this poem before Raja Parikshit. It is mentioned in it that the elephant, who was a king called Indradymna-a great devotee of Lord Vishnu in his earlier life, but owing to a curse had to take birth in the form of an elephant–gets trapped in the mire with its other leg held under the clutches of a deadly crocodile. When he was totally helpless, he let out this prayer for Lord Hari, who came to his rescue. This prayer describes very vividly all aspects of Lord Vishnu's personality, as conceived by the devotees. It is held by the devotees that its regular chanting with a feeling redeems one from even the most deadly trouble.

*(The translation is by the author of this book.)*

## The prayer: 'Gajendra-Moksha'
### (Redemption of The Elephant King)

Thus spake the sage Shukadeva1 Ji:

*Evam Vyavasito budhya samadhaa manohridi |*
*Jajaya paramam japyam pragjanmanyanushi kshitam || 1 ||*

Then steadying his wisdom with total concentration of his heart and mind, elephant recollected and chanted the following hymn, worth repeating, which he had learnt in his previous life ||1 ||

*Om namo Bhagvate tamsei yat etatchchidatmakam*
*Purushyadibeejaya pareshayabhideemahi || 2 ||*

He, with whose spirit this life-less body and mind gets energised with consciousness; who is represented by 'Om' the word, and who permeates all Nature and Beings—We rever that great God in our mind || 2 ||

*Yasminnidam Yatashchedam Yenedam Ya idam swayam |*
*Yoasmat parasmaccha paratam parpadye swayam-bhuvam || 3 ||*

He who creates and sustains this world and who is also manifest only through this world—I seek shelter in such Lord, self-created and beyond the scope of cause and effect || 3 ||

---

1. The son of the sage Vyas and narrator of Srimad Bhagwat.

*Yah swatmaneedam nijmayayapitam*
*Kwachidvibhatam Kwa cha tattirohitam |*
*Aviddhak sakshyubhyam tadeekshate*
*Sa atmamooloavatu mam paratparah || 4 ||*

He, who sees the apparent world—as defined by the scriptures, though created by his wish and who is visible in the time of existence and invisible in the period of dissolution, by his all pervading sight–and hence aloof from it–may He, the light of our vision protect me. || 4 ||

*Kalen panchatvamiteshu kritsnasho*
*Lokeshu paleshu cha sarvaheteshu |*
*Tamastadasseed gahanam gabheeram*
*Yastasya pareabhivirajate vibhuh || 5 ||*

Owing to the effect of time, all realms and all the guardians of the quarters like Brahma and others got dissolved in nature and only impregnable dark nature existed. But, beyond even that darkness, who ever remains lighted in his Super Realm, who is omniscient and ever radiant—may that Lord protect me. || 5 ||

*Na Yasya deva rishyah padam vidu—*
*rjantuh punah kaohartigantumeertum |*
*Yatha natasyakritibhivirche shtato*
*Duratyayanukramanah sa mavatu || 6 ||*

Like an actor performing various roles, is not recognised in reality by an ordinary viewer, the same way even the noble Gods and sages fail to realise, His real form, let alone the ordinary mortals. May God of such incomprehensible form, come to protect me. || 6 ||

*Didrikshavo yasya padam sumangalam*
*Vimuktasanga munyah susadhavah |*
*Charantyalokvritamvranam vane.*
*Bhootatmabhootah suhridah same gatih || 7 ||*

He, who is ever in total empathy with all the beings, free from mortal attractions; who is the well wisher of all and in the quest of getting whose vision before their eyes, the noble sages and saints perform great austerities while staying in jungles—may that God, be my ultimate goal. || 7 ||

*Na vidyate yasya cha janma karma va*
*Na namroope gunadosh eva va |*
*Tathapi lokapsy yasambhavaya yah*
*Swabhayaya tanyanukal mrichchhati || 8 ||*

He, who is neither born like we mortals owing to the destined deeds remaining undone, nor whose action has any arrogance of the doership, nor whose attributeless form has any name or entity but who creates and dissolves the whole world, out of a will in confirmity with his self-created norms || 8 ||

*Tasmei namah pareshayabrahmane ananta shaktaye |*
*Aroopayour oopaya nam ashcharyakarmane || 9 ||*

To Him, the All Powerful Supreme Lord, I bow in reverence to Him, formless yet with a myriad of shapes, the performer of amazing deeds—I repeatedly bow in reverence || 9 ||

*Nam atmapadeepaya sakshine parmatmane |*
*Namo giram vidooraya manasshchetasampati || 10 ||*

I bow to that Self-Lighted and Omnipresent Supreme. My repeated obeisance to that Lord, who is beyond the reach of mind, voice and attributes || 10 ||

*Sattven pratilabhyaya naishkaryena vipashchita |*
*Namah kaivalya nathaya nirvanasukhasancide || 11 ||*

My obeisance to Lord, who grants final release to men earning the right by their noble behaviour and who is the bliss of emancipation Himself || 11 ||

*Namah shantaya ghorya moodhaya gunadharmine |*
*Nirvisheshaya samyaya namo gyanghanaya cha ||12||*

My obeisance to Him, who appears quiet to those having the attributes, terrible to those having passionate attributes and impregnable to those having dull attributes. He is Immutable and Beacon of All Knowledge || 12 ||

*Kshetragyaya namastubhyam sarvadhuyakshaya sakshine*
*purushayatmamoolaya moolaprakritaye namah || 13 ||*

O Lord and creator of all body organs and senses and the very witness to their functioning—my obeisance to you! You, Lord, are Omniscient, the primal cause of nature but still beyond it—my reverence to you! || 13 ||

*Sarvendruiyagunadrashtre—sarvapratyayahetve*
*Asatachchhayayaktaya sadabhasaya te namah ||14||*

O! Master of all senses, the cause of all attractions! O! One present in all the worlds whether living or dead and appearing through all knowledge and ignorance (i.e., He is All In All)—my obeisance to You! ||14||

*Namo namastekhilakaranaya*
*Nishkarnayadbhutakaranaya |*
*Sarvagmamnaya maharnavaya*
*Namoapavargaya parayanaya ||15||*

You are the sole cause of everything but despite being the Cause, you are beyond Effect and hence unique–my repeated obeisance to you. O! the ultimate meaning of all the Vedas and Scriptures, the final destination of the salvation seeking noble men, the Lord Supreme—I bow the Thee! ||15||

*Gunaranichchhannachidooshmapaya*
*Tatkshobha visphoorjita mansaya |*
*Naishakarmya bhaven vivarjitagam*
*Swayam prakashaya namaskaromi ||16||*

He, who is hidden in all the three basic attributes of the creation like fire in the wood—it is an agitation in the attributes, that surfaces a desire of creation; who is ever radiant with the knowledge realised through austerities by nobles and saints—I bow to such Great Lord ||16||

*Madrikprapannapashupashavimokshnaya*
*Muktaya bhoori karunaya namoalayaya |*
*Swanshena sarvatanubhrinmanasi prateeta*
*Pratyagdrishe bhagwatevrihate namaste ||17||*

My obeisance to the Supreme Kind, ever-liberated Lord, who could rid me-an animal-of the noose of ignorance and who is never slow in shedding His mercy! Ever present through His spirit in the hearts of all beings, the ruler of All, the Lord Infinite—I bow to thee! ||17||

*Atmatmajaptagrihavittajaneshu sakte*
*rdushprapanaya guna sangavivarjhitaya |*

*Muktaumabhih swahriday paribhavitaya*
*Gyanatmne bhagwate namah Ishwaraya ||18||*

He, who is difficult to be realised by those infatuated with their bodies, friends, riches and family bonds and who is ever dwelling in the hearts of the liberated men, the Beacon of All knowledge and Omnipotent God–I bow to Thee! ||18||

*Yam dharmakamarthavimuktikama*
*Bhajant ishtam gatimapnuvanti |*
*Kim twareesho ratyaki dehamavyayam*
*Karotu meadabhradayo Vimokshanam ||19||*

He, who is approachable by those following their Dharma and who fulfils their all desires, including that of the final release, He also grants them unasked boons and imperishable body of His own attendant–that Supremely kind God may redeem me for ever from this trouble ||19||

*Ekantino yasya na kanchanarthey*
*vanchanti ye vei bhagavatprapannah |*
*Atyabhutam tachcharitam sumangalam*
*Gayanta anandasamudramagnah ||20||*

His loyal devotees, seeking shelter in His grace only, never desire for any material or spiritual benefit but only chant His auspicious glory of unique doings and thus remain ever immersed in the ocean of blessings. ||20||

*Tamaksharam Brahm param paresh*
*Mavyaktamadhyamikayogagamyam |*
*Ateendriyam sookshmamivatidoor*
*Manamtmadyam paripoornameede ||21||*

I bow to that Imperishable, Omnipresent, the Best, Ruler of all Gods including Brahma; Unmanifest for atheist but Manifest through deep devotion; despite being close, yet appearing very far owing to the veil of Illusion, Unrealisable through senses, Incomprehensible, Endless, yet the cause of every begining, and perfect in every way. ||21||

*Yusyu Brahmadayo deva Veda lokshcharcharah |*
*Namroopavibhedena phalgvya cha kalaya kritah ||22||*

With whose tiny fraction, are created all Gods including Brahma, the Four Vedas, the animate and inanimate world in myriad different forms ||22||

The rays of the burning fire and the shining sun repeatedly originating from their source and eventually again getting coalesced along with their wisdom and intellect get created by the self-Radiant God and also get coalesced with that Source only ||23||

*Sa vei na devasurmartyatiryan*
*Na stree na shandona puman na jantuh |*
*Nayam gunah karma na sanna chasan*
*Nishedhashesho jayatadasheshah ||24||*

That Lord is neither God, nor demon nor man nor of any sub-human species. Neither is He female nor male nor eunuch. Nor is He a being, not counted in the above mentioned categories. Neither is He an Attribute nor an Action nor a Cause. He is what remains after negating everything. He is that All in All. May that Lord incarnate Himself for redeeming me from this trouble ||24||

*Jijeevishe nahamihamuya ki*
*Mantarvahishchavritayebhayonya |*
*Ichchhami kalen na yasya viplava*
*Stasyatmaloka Varanasyamoksham ||25||*

I don't want to survive even after getting released from this crocodile's clutches because my pachydermatous body is covered with ignorance inside and out. I only crave redemption from that ignorance, which covers my soul and which does not get destroyed by the effect of time but only either by the divine grace or by the in-born enlightenment ||25||

*Soaham vishwarijam vishwamvishwam vishwa vedasam |*
*Viswatmanamajam Brahm pranatoasmi param padam ||26||*

Thus I crave shelter in, and give my obeisance to, that Exalted Supreme God, who creates the world and through his creation is Manifest Himself; all pervading yet aloof from it, playing with his Creation, Omnipresent and the best, that one could ever yearn for ||26||

*Yogarandhitakarmano hridi yogavibhavite |*
*Yogino Yam prapashyanti yogesham tam natoasmyyaham ||27||*

I bow to Him, the Lord, who is visualised by those, who have burnt their deeds in the fire of their unswearing devotion to Almighty. To that Almighty, I give my obeisance ||27||

*Namo namastubhyamasahyavega*
*Shaktitraayakhiladheegunaya |*
*Prapannapataya durantashaktaye*
*Kadinariyyanamanvapyavatarmane ||28||*

Whose powers delineating the three basic attributes (the noble, the passionate and the dull) have a tremendous speed to cope with, who appear as though He is the object satisfying all the sensual delights but to those sensual cravers, He is not accessible at all. My repeated obeisance to that protector of the shelter-seekers, the Immensely powerful Lord (you)! ||28||

*Namay Veda swamatmanam yakchaktyahm dhiyahatam |*
*Tam duratyayamahatmayam Bhagwantitoasmyaham ||29||*

He, whose illusive ignorance envelops the sense of the being, by the vain arrogance of the doership and prevents it from realising the reality—I seek shelter in that God of Infinite Grace. ||29||

Thus spake sage Sukdeva Ji;
*Evam Gajendramupavarnitanivirshesham*
*Brahmadayo vividhalingabhidabhimahnah |*
*Naite Yadoyasari purnikhhilatmakatvat*
*Tatrakhilamarmayo hariraviraseet ||30||*

When none of the Gods including Brahma-who deem various images to be in their real form-came for the rescue of the elephant, who was thus described the Integral form of Supreme Lord, the Supreme Lord, the Self same Lord Hari—who being the spirit, permeating all forms—appeared there. ||30||

*Tan tadvadrtta,i[a;anhya Jagnniwasah*
*Strotam nishibhya adivijaih sah sanstuvabhdih |*
*Chandomayena Garudena samuhyaman*
*Shohhakra yudhoaabhya gamdashu yato Gajendrah ||31||*

Seeing the big elephant, thus distressed and hearing the hymns recited by him, the weilder of the Disc Sudarshan, the Prop of the world, Lord rode on the back of Garuda, moving at will of his Master, reached near the elephant accompanied by Gods singing glories of the Lord. ||31||

*Soantssarasyuryubalen griheeta artto*
*Drishtwa Garutmati Hari Kha Upattachakam |*
*Utkshipya sambujakaram girimah Krichechhra*
*Nnaryanakhilguro Bhagwan Namaste ||32||*

When the elephant whose one feet was clutched by the teeth of a powerful crocodile, saw the Lord approaching in the sky astride Garuda, he raised his proboscis having a lotus, for God's worship and with great difficulty could utter: "O Lord Narayan, Adorable by all, I bow to Thee! ||32||

*Tan veekshya peeditamajah sahasavateertha.*
*Sagrahmashu sarasah kripayojjahar |*
*Trahad vipatitamukhadarina Gajendram*
*Sampashyatam Hariram-muchadusniyanam ||33||*

Seeing the elephant so distressed, Lord Hari quickly left Garuda and came down to the pond. His Supreme Kindness lifted the elephant alongwith the clutching crocodile and while the Gods watched in awe, Lord tore the jaws of the crocodile apart, as if in a trice, to release the elephant. ||33||

◻◻

# 18

## The Story of Naabhag And Ambreesha

Naabhag was the youngest son of Vaivaswata Manu. While Naabhag was still studying in a Gurukul (the school run by a sage), his brothers divided, among themselves, the entire property that their father had. When he returned completing his education, he was tersely told: "We have divided the entire property. Father has come in your share."

Unperturbed, Naabhag reached his father and said: "You alone have come in my share." Father, reassuring him, said: "Don't worry, my son. The brahmins of the Angiras Gotra are performing a yagya, closeby. But on every sixth day of the ceremony, they commit a mistake due to lack of their knowledge. You tell them the two sootka relating to the Vaishwadeva. When they would be going to the heaven, they would bequeath all of their property and riches to you."

Naabhag did the same. When the brahmins departed, they gave their entire wealth to him. But when he was gathering all the wealth, there appeared Rudradeva. He warned him: "This property belongs entirely to me. In case you have any doubt, you may go and confirm it from your father. He would guide you on the right path."

Naabhag went to his father. When he asked about the property, his father told him—"What Rudra Dev has told you is the truth. The progenitor, Daksha Prajapati, while laying down the rules for the Yagya, had proclaimed that the remainder of the Yagya property should be the right of Rudra only. Now you should go to Mahadeva (Rudra) and apologise for your mistake."

Naabhag returned quickly to Rudra Dev and hymned his glories. Then he said : "O Lord! Yagya's left over property truly, belongs to you only. I am sorry for having claimed it. Please forgive me."

Lord Rudra was happy with his honesty. He said: "You are truly wise. Now I will give all that is my share in any Yagya". Saying so, he disappeared. Naabhag got the reward of his honesty. He lived happily, thereafter.

He had a son called Ambreesha, who was an ardent devotee of the Supreme Lord Hari. He was so pure, that no curse from even the most pious Brahmin could have touched him. He was a very patient and noble ruler. He used worship his chosen Lord Vishnu. Lord Vishnu had asked his Sudarshan Chakra to always ensure his security. Raja Ambreesha's wife was also a very religious minded and devout lady.

Once the king with his queen, took a vow of piously keeping the fast on every Ekadashi, which was to be broken on the following day after a ritual worship. When his fast come to an end, worshipped Lord Hari and invited the brahmins to a feast. After feeding them, he donated also a variety of alms to the brahmins. When he was about to take his food–there arrived, all of a sudden, the fiery sage, Durvasa. The king got up to offer him an exalted seat and devotedly welcomed him. Then the king requested the sage to have his food. Durvasa, had actually come to test the king's faith in his belief in Lord Hari. He said: "O King! I'd have my food only when I have taken my bath in the river close by and after doing my routine worship."

The King decided to wait for the sage's return, as it would have been a sacrilege if he had taken his food before Durvasa. But the sage took a long time and didn't return. The time to break fast was fast approaching. When the appointed hour arrived the king could do nothing. He was helpless to break his fast. As he was eating his food, there arrived Durvasa. Learning that the King had already taken his food, Durvasa lost his temper. Enraged he created a deadly Kritya (an evil spirit), which came charging at Ambreesha. But all of a sudden, a huge discuss–the Chakra Sudarshana–appeared there revolving constantly around the king's seat and preventing the Kritya from reaching close to him. Their battle ensued for long and at last, resignedly, the Kritya turned back and boomeranged on the sage himself. This is the rule, with the evil spirits. If they fail to accomplish the job they have been created for, they invariably return and destroy their creator.

Now Durvasa panicked. He was not used to this, as he had almost never been on the receiving end of any wrath. He fled for his safety. Right from Brahma to Lord Shiva, he visited every God but they expressed their inability to protect him from that Kritya. Eventually he sought shelter in Vaikuntha, only to be told that only Raja Ambreesha and no else could provide him the relief. Durvasa returned to the king, with that Kritya still on his hot pursuit. He reached close to the King and fell flat before him with a cry: "Protect me from this deadly Kritya. Else it would kill me."

Ambreesha, the wise and patient King, rose up from his throne and stood hand bound and head-bowed before that spirit. As he did so, the Kritya vanished and Durvasa heaved a sigh of relief. Then he apologised before the king: "I'm truly sorry to have dared to show my wrath before the devotee of Vishnu." The King bowed gracefully and said: "You are Kind Sage!" The sage, then, also gave him a boon: " Henceforth I proclaim that all the true devotees of Vishnu, like you are, shall be beyond the effect of any evil spirit and no unreasonable wrath can even touch them."

◻◻

# 19

# King Dushyanta And Bharata

Puru's dynasty produced many noble saintly kings and Dushyanta was one of them. He was a very powerful and popular king. One day, he left on his hunting expedition with his companions. But misled by a possible prey, he was separated from his colleagues. And moving astray, he happened to reach sage Kanva's hermitage, quite unknowingly. He was thirsty and he wanted water. Spotting a dwelling place, he came close to it and saw a beautiful girl plucking flowers. On demand she gave him some water. The king had fallen in instant love with that captivating girl. Although the girl had introduced her as the daughter of sage Kanva, Dushyanta asked the girl: "O Dame! You are not a brahmin girl for all I know. You surely have some different charms."

Shakuntala replied: "I admire your deep insight to reveal a person's character by appearance. In any case, you are right. I am the daughter of Sage Vishwamitra and the divine dancer Menaka. But since Sage Kanva reared me up, I deem only him as my father." Whereupon, the king, madly in love, proposed to marry her after revealing his identity. Now, King Dushyanta was a well known king and any girl would have felt honoured at receiving the proposal. Although the sage raised some objections, seeing Shakuntala's love for the king, Kanva also consented. Their marriage was solemnised in the 'Gandharava- Marriage' category according to which the willing adults can always marry.

After staying there for some time and enjoying the imptial bliss in the company of Shakuntala, Dushyant decided to leave. He said that soon he would return and left a ring with Shakuntala as his souvenir. "This is your mark of identification for me. Till you have this, I shall never forget you. Soon we'll meet."

Only within few days of the king's departure, Shakuntala realised that she was pregnant. Meanwhile, she had heard nothing from Dushyanta. While she was thinking of sending a messenger or going herself to remind the king of his promise, one day, she went to take bath in the river and the ring accidentally slipped from her finger and fell into the water. Though she tried, she couldn't get back the ring. At last resignedly, she returned home, began preparing for the journey to the capital. But what she didn't realise was that after losing her identification mark, how the king would recognise her? Never the less, accompanied by Kanva's disciple, she left.

But the king refused to recognise her. Though much she pleaded, the absence of the identification mark couldn't make her convince the king, that she was her wife. At last, she had to return and continue living in sage Kanva's hermitage. At due time, she produced a robust son. Right from the childhood, he was very brave and intelligent. Kanva gave him the name 'Bharata¹" and completed his all ceremonies, in accordance with the kshatriya customs. Bharat was so brave that lions and tigers were like pet cats to him.

Meanwhile, after much toil Shakuntala got back her lost ring. In fact it was swallowed by a fish and, having netted it, when the fisherman slit its stomach, he got that ring. Since he knew the sage and all about Shakuntala, he went to the hermitage to return the ring. Shakuntala was delighted to get it back.

One day Dushyant happened to come to the same jungle. At the periphery of the holy cottage, he found a robust but tender aged boy moving astride a lion with a tiger following him tamely. Amazed, he enquired about the boy and this enquiry led him to the hermitage. Since by then Shakuntala had received her lost ring, Dushyanta recognised her immediately. He was delighted to learn that the robust boy Bharat was his own son. Happily, he brought them to the capital and at due time, appointed Bharat as the King. King Bhart was truly unassailable overlord of this entire region. No King had the power to defy his orders. He performed as many as 55 Ashwamedha Yagyas on the bank of Ganga and 78 on the bank of Yamuna. At his time, he was the king

---

1. Generally it is believed that Bharatvarsha (literally meaning a big chunk of land named after Bharata) is the name derived from this Bharata's name.

emperor of the entire earth.

Bharata had three sons but he deemed all of them to be unfit to be a ruler. In order to get a better son, he performed the Yagya called 'Marutasoma'. The Marugana were pleased and they gave him a son called Bharadwaj, whose story of origin is also quite interesting.

Once the divineGuru Brihashpati felt so much charged with the desire for copulation that he even forced his younger brother's Utathya's wife, who was already pregnant, to have sex with him. But when he was prevented by the son inside the womb from committing this sin, Brihaspati, mad in his lust, cursed that yet-to be-born to go blind. And then he copulated with Utathay's wife. This resulted in her miscarriage and while conceiving for the second time, when she was afraid that she might be deserted by her husband, Brihaspati reassured her: "Don't worry. This boy shall be known as my, as well as, Utathya's son and be called as Bhardwaj (literally filled or created by two persons."

◻◻

# 20

## Raja Rantideo's Hospitality

Bharadwaj continued the lineage of Bharat. It was in this dynasty that Raj Rantideo was born. He was a committed fatalist by nature. He never earned anything and never hesitated from donating whatever he had. That was why, his financial condition deteriorated and his whole family was left starving for 48 days at a stretch. But he was a very patient person and devoid of any infatuation. It was only on the 49th day that he could procure some rice, ghee (clarified butter), curds and the food was cooked with great gusto. But as the family was about to partake of the food after 48 days starvation, there arrived suddenly a brahmina guest. Now the hospitable king didn't hesitate for a moment and fed that brahmina first. Rantideo gave the entire left-over food to that person and his dogs. Now he thought that he should, at least, have some water. But then came a thirsty pariah and he gave the entire water to him. While doing all this, he felt greatly happy and supremely satisfied. And lo and behold! There appeared a vimana carrying Lord Hari, Brahma and Shiva. It was actually these three Gods, who appeared in various forms of the brahmina and the pariah etc. to test his faith in God. And Rantideo emerged with flying colours. Soon he was taken to heaven and Lord Hari eventually merged his soul into his Supreme Spirit.

His name is often quoted to show the high standard of hospitality in this entire region.

It was in this very family that Ahalya, the wife of Gautam sage, who was redeemed from her curse of petrifaction, was born.

# 21

# The Descent of The Ganga

That the river Ganga had its origin from Lord Vishnu's feet and it continued to flow in heaven have already been referred to, but how it came on to the earth is an interesting story.

In the family of veridicious Raja Harishchandra,[1] was born Sagar. Raja Harishchandra's great grandson was Badaka. When Badaka died, his wife was pregnant. Though she wanted to be a Sati (burning herself at the pyre after dead husband), all the seniors of the family and the sages advised against it, since in that event one more life would have been destroyed. However, when king's other wives learnt about her being in a family way, out of sheer jealously they poisoned her. But it was God's will, that no ill effect of the poison could even touch that boy in the womb. Since he was born with that poison nullified, he was called 'Sagar' which literally means with poison. When he came of age, he proved to be a dominant ruler. He had 60,000 sons. Once he performed the Ashwamedha Yagya.

He sent the consecrated horse ahead and asked his sons to protect the horse and defeat any one who dared to challenge the horse's entry. The entry of the horse into any region, signified the region accepting the authority of the king who performed that Yagya. As the horse moved, Indra felt jealous of the might Raja Sagar, might command and so he stole the horse. All the 60,000 sons of Raja Sagar searched the horse but they couldn't find it. They even went inside the earth to search that horse. Meanwhile, fearing to be identified as the thief of the consecrated horse,

---

[1]. The Story in details has also been given in the Devi Bhagwat Purana of the same series.

**Indra** quietly left it tied in sage Kapil' hermitage based in the nether world. When the 60,000 sons of Raja Sagar, saw the horse tied there with a sage lost in meditation, they thought the culprit was the sage Kapil. Their shouts and yells disturbed the sage's concentration, who opened his eyes angrily and his fiery gaze incinerated all the sons of Sagar in an instant.

When they didn't return, Raja Sagar sent his other son, called Asamanjas, from his other wife, to search them.

He also reached Kapil sage's hermitage and there he saw the heaps of the dead bodies. When he learnt that those were the bodies of his father's lost 60,000 sons and the reason for their death, he prayed Sage Kapil to be pleased with him. He also apologised on his dead step brothers' behalf. Then Kapil told him: "Now they would have their salvation only, when the divine river Ganga comes on to the earth to wash down their bodies."

Getting this hint, Asamanjas told his father, who initiated a massive project to make Ganga descend on to the earth and after Sagar, Asmanjas, then his son Anshuman and Anshuman's son, Dilip, also kept on trying to make Ganga descend on to the earth. However, it was Dilip's son Bhagirath, whose devout penance pleased Ganga as much as to make her agree to coming down to the earth. But Ganga said: "When I descend, because of my sheer force I may penetrate the earth and go down. So you must have some one to break my fall. Perhaps only Lord Shankar can do so." The Bhagiratha started worshipping Lord Shankar. He agreed to take the burden. But in order to remove Ganga's arrogance about her force, he made Ganga fall on to his hair and get lost in his locks. Bhagirath again, requested Lord Shiva to release it. When it started flowing on to the earth, it flowed with such a force that sage Jahnu's entire hermitage capsized under its force. The sage became so angry, as to drinkup the river entirely. Again Bhagirath had to request sage Jahnu, who agreed to release Ganga from a slit made in his thigh. Then Ganga flowed with serenity and in a

---

1. The place where the Ganga confluences with the sea (Bay of Bangal).

stream line. Bhagirath led its way by travelling ahead of it in a chariot. Eventually it was taken to sage Kapil's hermitage at Ganga Sagar[1]. Reaching there Ganga washed Bhagirath's forefathers' dead bodies to ensure salvation to their souls.

[Perhaps immersing 'ashes' in the Ganga water is the tradition that started with this event.]

# 22

# Marriage of Vasudeva And Devaki

As the Dwaper Age set in, the Dharma lost its two legs[1] and unrighteous order became increasingly rampant. Many demons appeared on the earth as the rulers, further making the conditions on the earth more adverse. The Earth was getting increasingly distressed. So, assuming the form of a cow, she went to Brahma with the hope of getting some succour. Hearing her tale of woe, Brahma thought it was time Lord Hari was invoked. With this intention, he began to chant the holy 'Purush-Sookta' to invoke the Supreme Lord. Gods, who were also getting weak and emaciated due to not receiving their oblations as the Yagya had ceased to be performed, also joined in prayer with Brahma. While they were devotedly praying, they heard a divine voice telling them: "Worry not, O gods and the Earth! The Blessed Lord would soon incarnate as the son of the Vasudeva in Shaursaini family of the Yadu dynasty." He advised all Gods to appear in that dynasty to render their support in restoring the righteous order on the earth.

Gods, Brahma and the Earth felt greatly reassured. Delighted by the possibility of seeing the Blessed Lord soon, they all returned to their realms and started preparations to descend on to the Earth.

Mathura, at that time was the capital of Yadu's descendants. The scions of the Bhojvansha, Devaka had a daughter called Devaki. He married her off to Vasudeva, the son of Shoorsena. Her brother (cousin) was Kansa, who was a very powerful person. He had put his father, Ugarsena, into prison and assumed the rulership of Mathura.

When Vasudeva was going home on his chariot driven by Kansa, suddenly a heavenly voice boomed: "O Kansa! Your this sister's eighth issue shall cause your death."

---

1. Dharma or the religious duty loses its potency as time heads towards final Dissolution, according to Srimadbhagwat Purana.

Kansa was bewildered for a moment. But then regaining his composure, he decided to eliminate his sister, the future mother of his potential death-cause. He held Devaki by her hair and was about to kill her, when Vasudeva requested him to let go his wife. " I promise to deliver all our issues at your door-step, to enable you slaying them. But, please don't kill my wife." Kansa thought for a moment and then instead of taking the chariot toward the palace, turned it towards the royal prison of Mathura. He never wanted the couple escaping and then producing a son who might slay him.

In due course of time seven, male issues were born to Devaki and as per the promise Vasudeva brought each of them to Kansa, who killed all of them mercilessly. When Devaki became pregnant for the eighth time, she was over-whelmed with happiness and apprehension simultaneously. She was joyful, as she realised that Lord Supreme had come in her womb but, at the same time, she feared that Kansa would kill her eighth son also.

Although Devaki's only eighth issue was destined to kill Kansa, the latter decided to kill all her issues relaying on Narad's advice. Narad, on hearing the prophesy, advised Kansa: " O King! It is difficult to say which shall be the eighth issue. Counting from the end, even the first could be the eighth issue in case your sister produces only eight issues." Getting confused with this advice, Kansa decided to kill all the issues of Devaki.

□□

# 23

# Incarnation of Lord Krishna And Other Events

So, on the eighth lunar day of the month of Bhadrapada (15th August or 15 Sept., nearly), precisely, at twelve at night the eighth son of Devaki was born. But an unusual happening accompanied his birth. Just a few moments before his birth, all the doors of the prison opened automatically and the guard dozed off, uncontrollably. Getting the divine hint, Vasudeva decided to take the new-born across the river Yamuna to his friend Nanda's house. A divine voice suggested to Vasudeva, to exchange the boy with the daughter born in Nanda's house, exactly at the moment his son was born.

As he took the child into a wicker basket and placed the basket upon his head, the river began to swell meaningfully. It also started raining heavily. Carefully, Vasudeva entered the river with that basket containing the child over his head because the depth of the river had began to increase. And the moment Yamuna arose as much as to touch the feet of the son, and then, it began to subside as if by magic. The river, perhaps, wanted to touch the feet of the Lord.

Then Vasudeva conveniently crossed the river and reached Nanda's house on the other bank of the river. To his surprise, he found the gates of the house wide open and he entered in. Quietly taking away the daughter delivered by Yashoda and placing his own son besides her instead, Vasudeva quickly came out and wading through Yamuna, he reached back the prison, near Devaki. As he returned inside, the doors of the prison automatically closed and the guards on duty again woke up. Hearing the cry of the new born child, they immediately informed their king, Kansa. Kansa came and took away the baby, neglecting mercilessly the entreaties of his sister. As Kansa tried to dash the new born child, who was a girl, against the prison wall, she slipped from his hand and rose up to the sky. Then a booming divine voice informed Kansa. "You rogue! Your Kal[1]

---

1. The cause of death.

has already taken birth! You can't escape your destiny!" And then the new born girl also vanished in the sky.

[*Some versions say that Devaki's seventh child also lived on having escaped Kansa's wrath. It is believed that the seventh child was the incarnation of the Serpent-Shesh, on whose coil the Blessed Lord Vishnu rests. Knowing Kansa's intention, Vishnu, with his divine sleight managed to transplant the embryo to Vasudeva's another wife, Rohini's womb who lived with Nanda. In due time, the child was born and came to be known as Balrama or Haldhar as he always carried a replica of a plough upon is shoulder.*]

When the girl Yogamaya–as she is called and worshipped– vanished into the skies, Kansa was furious. Despite all precautions, he couldn't slay his potential slayer. Kansa, therefore, ordered his demons and wicked hench persons to kill every child, who had just been born. But despite his efforts, Krishna, survived and began to grow up with his elder brother Balarama in Gokula.

## The Episode of Pootana

The people of Vraja-kshetra were distressed by Kansa's vile order to slay all the new-born children. Yashoda, who didn't know that Krishna was actually not her son but, of Devaki, was also worried. Often she was bewildered by her son's strange behaviour. One moment he would appear as the usual baby but the very next moment he would appear as the Lord of Universe. Moreover, she was panicky after having heard Kansa's cruel order. But despite her care, the demons kept on coming to slay her child although they couldn't succeed.

Once Kansa sent the vampire-nurse called Pootana to destroy him. She changed herself into a beautiful and charming woman and reaching Nanda's home took the child on her knee and tried to feed him. She had her breast-nipple covered with a deadly poison. But Krishna took the nipple of her breast inside his mouth and sucked it so forcefully, as to draw life out of her. Pootana fell to the ground assuming her real shape, horrifying the people, who thought her to be a simple loving woman.

[According to an ancient legend, there was a daughter of the Demon Lord Bali, called Ratnamala. Seeing Bhagwan Vaman (the Dwarf Incarnation) present in the Yagya Venue, she longed to have him as her son. Vamana realised her wish and fulfilled it in her this life when she was born as Pootana. Her longing to feed the Lord was fulfilled.]

When the Gops[1] saw the spectacle of a dominoes lying dead with Krishna playing upon her breast, they quickly took the child away. Then a nervous Yashoda bathed her child in the urine of cow to ward off any evil influence around him. The people of the area hacked off the dead body of Pootana into pieces. When they burnt it, it emanated a sweet incense's smell. Vasudeva thanked God gratefully for having protected his infant child's life.

## Shakatasura And Trinavarta

At another time, a demon, called Shakatasura attempted to destroy Krishna. One day Yashoda was playing with the child, Krishna, when she was called away and so that Krishna should remain safe, she left him under an old bullock-cart in the yard. That demon in the form of the cart, made an attempt to have the cart fall over Krishna and kill him. But child, the incarnation of the Lord of Universe, sensed the demon's designs and lifting with his toe, threw that cart on the other side of the yard and the demon was instantly killed.

Once when the child Krishna and Yashoda were together, a black cloud came menancingly and covered them from sight, and when it left, Yashoda saw the child hanging on to the throat of that cloud demon and being swept along by it. It looked as if nothing could save him. As she watched, full of terror, a bull came over and the cloud floated slowly into the village with the tiny child still holding his throat. Later on people found that cloud demon–called Trinavarta–lying dead, with the child Krishna merrily playing upon his dead body.

## Vrittasura And Dhenukasura

Meanwhile, Kansa continued to worry about his killer and plotted constantly to kill Krishna, the child repeatedly. One day, Krishna and Balarama were playing on the bank of the river Yamuna. They were there

---

1. The boys attending cows.

to look after their cows and calves grazing there. By taking the shape of a calf, then, came a demon called Vrittasura intending to kill the brothers. The demon owing to his form, could easily mingle with the other calves. Krishna, however, especially noticed this and he immediately alerted Balarama about the presence of a demon. Both the brothers followed him and pounced upon him. Krishna, caught hold of the demon calf by two hind legs of the beast and tail, swing him around forcefully and threw him up into a tree.

Krishna also killed Dhenukasura in Talavana, a picturesque spot near a pond. This forest was full of toddy trees. The demon Dhenukasura (the demon in the form of a donkey) lived there and so it was difficult for people to go for picking up fruits etc. The ferocious donkey attacked Krishna and Balarama with great force, shaking the whole field. Then Balarama caught hold of the legs of the donkey with one hand and wheeling him round, threw him into the tree tops.

## Bakasura And Kaliya Episode

Another day at the bank of river Yamuna, Krishna saw a huge duck as big as a hill. It was Bakasur (the duck-demon), as powerful as a thunder-boat. He was a friend of Kansa, and he attacked Krishna with his pointed sharp beaks and quickly swallowed him up, but Bakasur felt a burning, and fiery sensation in his throat. This was due to the growing heat created by Krishna. The demon quickly disgorged Krishna up and tried to kill him by pinching him in the beak. But Krishna caught hold of the beak of the gigantic duck and split its beak, just as a child easily splits a blade of grass.

However, no sooner than Krishna was through, taking on Bakasura and killing him eventually, that he encountered another difficulty. A demon came assuming the shape of a very fat python. Then he stretched his mouth open like a mountain cave, desiring to swallow Krishna, and all the cowherd boys. The Python devoured all the cows and cowherd boys, who were all sucked into the python's mouth. Seeing this, Krishna also entered it and expanded his size so enormously that the python was burst and all the cowherd boys and the cows were released.

Krishna used to go with calves and cows on the bank of Yamuna for feeding the cows and playing. In the deep pit inside the river, there lived Kaliya serpent which emanated poisonous vapours, causing death to many cows etc. which happened to drink from Yamuna's bank. Due to that poisonous effect, all the trees around had shrivelled and dried up. One day, while playing with a ball with his companions, Krishna happened to accidentally throw the ball into the Yamuna's polluted water. Since the ball belonged to his friend, Manasukha, the latter adamantly demanded his ball back. Then Krishna took up the challenge and jumped into the river having the den of Kaliya. He made a lot of noise in the water to wake the dreadful Kaliya up. Getting enraged, the serpent came before Krishna and entangled the boy into the coils of his many hoods.

The news of Krishna jumping into the den of Kaliya spread all-around like wild fire. All the people around became panicky after getting the news and they rushed to Yashoda and Nanda to apprise them of the dangerous bid, that Krishna had made. They too rushed to the spot on the bank. But feeling totally helpless to bring their darling from that serpent's den— the people had wisely prevented them from even going near the water for the sake of their own lives—the worrying parents had no go but to pray God. But in about a couple of hours, they saw their beloved Krishna emerging out of the water, perched on the hoods of Kaliya with the ball in his hand. He had tamed the ferocious serpent after a fight and ordered it to leave the pit for ever with his family, else Krishna would slay all of them. Kaliya bowed to the order and then Krishna triumphantly emerged out of water.

## Other Events

Krishna's feats continued to serve the interest of the oppressed. Though he was just a lad, his such feats made him supremely popular even when he was just a kid. He also killed the demon Pralambasura, when this demon tried to take away Balarama. Once he also devoured the forest fire to protect the herd of cows.

Once Krishna embarrassed all the virgins of the region, by hiding their clothes on a tree when they were taking bath in the river Yamuna, with not even a shred of cloth upon their person. In fact this was a ritual observed by the unmarried girls of the Vraja region, prior to their worshipping the Goddess Katyayani. After shedding their clothes, they would take bath in Yamuna and then they would go to the temple totally unclad to worship the Goddess and pray to be blessed with the husband of their choice. Although that 'Ghat' was in a secluded spot, nevertheless, it was a public place and taking bath unclad was surely indecent. Krishna managed to sneak in the spot and perched himself at a high tree almost at the edge of the water of the river, with the girls' clothes bundle close to him. The girls, when they began to come out of water, found their clothes missing. Feeling uncomfortable, they entered the river again. Then they saw Krishna sitting on a tree with their clothes. At last, Krishna returned their clothes only after ensuring their not indulging in this indecent ritual any more. This 'leela' (sportive play) of Krishna is called the 'Cheera-harana leela.'

## Goverdhan-Worship

As Krishna grew up, he tried to educate his people by making them shed many useless customs. One of them was making the people stop the worship of Indra. The Brahmin priests used to make the people of Vraj worship Indra on the day following Deepavali, as a thanks giving ceremony of the Gods' chief for having provided them with good rains. Krishna told them that it was not rain alone that was responsible for good crop but their own labour and the toil of their animals. He made them feed to their cows and bullocks and intelligently plan the water resource management by making dams etc. It is believed that he made people construct a dam near the mount called Goverdhan. There, on the appointed day, all the material that was to be used in Indra's worship, was fed to the bullocks and cows etc. and they also worshipped the mount Goverdhan, which provided to the people of the area resemblance of a bullmark against the deluging waters of the rivers and small water courses.

When Indra detected this insult, he ordered dense-dark clouds to surround the Vraja area and submerge it in the heavy rains causing water courses to swell. So it happened and the people were stressed by this form of the nature. But Krishna provided them a safe shelter near the

Goverdhan mount and Indra couldn't destroy them or their cattle-stock. Allegorically this event is described as the Lord Krishna lifting the mount on his small finger (i.e. making much less efforts) and providing shelter to all the distressed people and the cattle-stock, beneath the raised up mount. When Indra saw his wrath causing no harm to the people of Vraja, he came down begging pardon from Krishna, whom he recognised as no else but the incarnated form of the blessed Lord Hari. Not only the divine chief came hand-bound to apologise but he promised to provide better natural services to the people of that area. This 'Leela' of Krishna is called 'Goverdhan Leela'.

## His Other Feats

Krishna's deeds earned him many admirers and while he was hardly in his teens, he had become the local hero. His glory tended to grow.

One day when Krishna and Balarama went to forest and were absorbed in music and dance, a demon named Shankasur appeared on the scene. The two brothers quickly followed the demon, whose head resembled a counch shell. Krishna caught him, stuck his head with his fists and killed him. It was only he, who also liberated the earth from the burden of the demons called Arishthasura and Kesi.

Once, when Krishna was enjoying his dance and singing amidst the company of the Gopis, there arrived a Yaksha called Shankhachood. He entered the group, when their music and dance were inching toward ecstasy, which had made the Gopis drenched in sweat and their clothes were also getting lose. The Yaksha tried to elope with the Gopis, when Krishna identified him and killed him with his one powerful fisty blow. When it fell on to the ground, the crown-jewel embedded in his head emerged out at the impact. Krishna lifted it and presented it to his brother Balarama.

## Enchanting Flute Player

Apart from killing the demons and educating people, Krishna also entranced the Gopis with his loving pranks and his superlative command over flute playing. At the time of full moon, the sound of Krishna's flute would reach the cow's & maidens' ears and leaving, whatever they were busy in, they would rush madly to the source of the flute sound. When all of them would come together, the great Raas'[1] dance would commence. In this each Gopi would have Krishna's company, as if he was not one but many. And at the peak of the ecstatic dance and music, he would just vanish, leaving them blaming each other for taking him away from their midst. His pranks with Gopis, at the time of Holi festival are many which, have become an inseparable part of our culture.

## Krishna Defies Kansa

Krishna also made his people defy the order from Kansa, that all milk and butter should be first sent to Mathura and after the 'royal-cut' the remaining part might be consumed by the producer of the milk and milk products. This was in fact, tantamount to fleecing the people of the region, where the main product was not agricultural products like cereal or grain, but milk. In order to encourage people stop the milk's compulsory supply to Mathura, he himself started looting or eating the milk and its products, taken by the Gopis to Mathura. Also, in order to protect the supply remaining within the region he started, with his friends, to secretly enter the houses of Gopis and eat their butter and milk. This earned him yet another epithet, Makhan-Chor, for which his mother used to frequently scold him. But this was his style of defying the royal order of Kansa.

One day, in order of restrict Krishna's movement Yashoda tied him with a rope to the heavy axle of a cart-wheel and left him to play within the restricted area. But that tiny boy playfully draft the heavy axle along while passing through the two trees standing close to each other. He forced his way between them, until the axle was wedged between those trees. Then, with a pull, he passed through and the trees fell down with a loud crash. Two shining spirits appeared before him. They said they had been imprisoned in the trees, until Krishna could release them and in gratitude, they offered him their oblation and worship.

---

1. Literally meaning the fount of Raas which means the ultimate relish of any enjoyment.

## Universe In Krishna's Mouth

One day Krishna swallowed some clay. But when the mother told him to open his mouth, she saw there not the clay but the whole Universe. All the stars, planets, galaxies and their movements as well. She was bewildered. But immediately the "Leela Purushottam" [The Sportive Man Par Excellence] displaying his pranks, withdrew his maya and the mother saw his mouth becoming absolutely normal.

Another time she tied his hands together with a churning rope to keep him out of mischief. But, though she tied together all ropes she could not make one, long enough to get round his small wrists. When she began to despair, Krishna suddenly let her tie his wrists with a piece of string!

☐☐

# 24

## Kansa Dethroned And Destroyed

While Krishna was in Gokul, Kansa continued to send his agents in various forms to Krishna, but they all failed. At last on the pretence of seeing the physical prowess of these lads from Gokula, Kansa sent Akroora, his trusted lieutenant, to bring Krishna and Balaram to Mathura to attend big wrestling competition.

Akroora, with a royal invitation reached the house of Nanda Baba. Getting the news, the whole of village including the nearby areas plunged into doom. But Krishna knew that the hour of final reckoning was round the corner. So, despite a flood of protest from every side, he left for Mathura in Akroora's chariot with Balarama.

When they arrived in Mathura, the other Gops (cowherds' men and Krishna's friends) stayed in the periphery while Krishna and Balarama went though the city and came to the place prepared for wrestling competition. On the way, as they came close, a mad elephant, was let loose on the two brothers, notorious for its power and quick temper, the pachyderm menancingly came charging at them. But undaunted, the two brothers held it in check and slayed it in no time.

The next day all were ready for the competition as Kansa took his royal seat. He made his two trusted wrestlers, named Mushtik and Channor come to face the two brothers. The professional wrestlers had received the secret royal instructions to defeat the brothers to death. But as the bout began, it happened the other way round. In no time, two lads eliminated them and then killed the wrestlers. This made Kansa rise up to shout orders to his soldiers to arrest the two brothers.

Seizing his time while Balarama checked the advancing troops, Krishna leapt to the royal seat and held Kansa by crown hair of his head and after which he kicked his crown. Then Krishna dashed him against the ground the same way, as Kansa had dashed the former's six brothers and a sister. Kansa was eventually killed, to the great delight of the Gods and noble persons.

When the order was restored, the funeral rites for the deceased king were prepared, Krishna himself set the fire to the pyre. He also comforted the bereaved queen and put Kansa's father, Ugrasen–whom Kansa had imprisoned–on the throne again, and set his own parents, Vasudeva and Devaki free. They were thrilled to see their son after such a long gap. The whole Mathura rejoiced, getting rid of the tyrant ruler in the form of Kansa.

❏❏

# 25

## Krishna Outwits Brahma

Much before Krishna's advent to Mathura to dethrone and destroy Kansa, he had even outwitted the Creator. He was hardly five years old then.

Once with his friends, Krishna went to the bank of Yamuna, where all of them felt hungry. Since they had the 'Kaleva' (snacks to be consumed out of home) with them, they decided to consume it after their exhaustive games. First they played there and then took a lazy bath in the river of Yamuna. This further whetted their appetite and they felt famished. Without waiting for the edibles to be laid properly on the leaf-plates, they started eating from tiny boxes and pitchers which they had brought along, full of eatables like butter, whey and cereal preparations. They had their merry time in eating the choicest preparations made by their friends' mothers.

Brahma couldn't resist the temptation of seeing his Super Lord indulging in a playful mood with his friends. Since he found all the cowherd boys indifferent to their cattle stock– going far away while grazing, Brahma, in a playful zest, stole the calves and cows and hid them in a deep cave. Suddenly Mansukha became aware about it and he scolded Krishna: "It is because of your spell-binding pranks that we became indifferent to our cows and calves. Now they are not visible here. We must go to find them. Else we can't dare return home for the fear of getting a severe drubbing by our elders."

Then, led by Krishna, the search party, licking still the butter and sugar-candy smeared fingers, went out to search their cattles. Brahma seized the opportunity to hide the Gwalas (the cow herd boys) in the same cave, when they went a little away from Krishna. Now Krishna was worried. But immediately he learnt through his Yogic power, the trick that Brahma had played upon him. With a smile, he recreated the exact replicas of the lost boys, cows and calves, with no one detecting the difference.

When it was dusk time, they all returned home. Even the parents of the lost boys and the owners of the cows and calves could not find any thing amiss. And curiously enough, the cowherd women, with their sons recreated by Krishna's Yogic power, became all the more affectionate to their sons without realising the difference. It was because, sub-consciously they might have felt greater affection to their sons since they had been re-created at Krishna's own behest, though they couldn't feel the difference. However, Balarama detected that something was truly amiss. One day, he closed his eyes and concentrated inwardly. Lo and behold, he found every thing in Vraja, the women, men, boys, girls, cattles, trees and was startled with the overwhelming presence of Krishna. Krishna appeared to him every where. When he asked Krishna about his vision, the latter told: "Dauoo! (elder Brother)! It is Brahma who created this mischief. It is to outwit him, that I wrought this spectacle."

This way a full year passed by but the Vraja-vasis (the dwellers of Vraja) couldn't detect any difference. They felt everything in order. Brahma, when saw the Vraja totally unchanged, was bewildered. He wanted to dupe the boy Krishna, who outwitted the Creator so smartly. At last he concentrated his mind on Krishna and prayed: "O Lord! Show me your presence in this area. I am keen to see you in your childhood from." And a smiling Krishna appeared, with the crown of the peacock feather and his favourite flute, licking his hands smeared with butter and sugar-candy mixture. He was exactly in this form, when Brahma tried to dupe him a year ago. Then alighting from his vehicle, the Swan, Brahma bowed his head lovingly and reverentially going around Krishna, and left for his realm totally outwitted by a mere boy!

☐☐

# 26

# Krishna and Balrama Feel Hungry

Once while grazing the cows, both the brothers felt hungry. Krishna said to Balarama. "Dauoo! I am feeling famished. You are more powerful and elder to me. It is your duty to procure some food for me."

"But where to find in this jungle?" questioned Balarama. Then Krishna suggested: "A little away, on the bank of Yamuna, some brahmins of Mathura are performing a quiet Yagya. Send some of our boys to get from them, some edibles. They must be having plenty of them as no Yagya ceremony is completed without the accompanying feast."

When the boys went to the brahmins, they contemptuously said: "Even before the oblation is fed to the Gods, you want food to be given to you! Are you all nonsense? Don't come here, till our Yagya is completed. Else we shall beat you and scare you away."

Resignedly, the cowherd boys began to return. A little far away from spot where the male-fold were sitting, the women of those brahmins were preparing food for the feast. When they heard that some boys were hungry and wanted food, they quickly prepared few plates, filled with the choicest edibles and left, to feed the boys and their companions. When their husbands objected, they didn't listen to them. At last, they managed to reach near Balarama, Krishna and other boys, guided by the boy-messengers and fed them food to their great satisfaction. Whereupon Krishna told them: "O noble ladies! We are delighted by the affection you have showered on us, by offering us the best possible food. Now you better go back to your husbands as they won't be able to complete the Yagya in your absence. But we bless you that if your male-folk keep their treasure confined to your possession, it shall ever increase. But the moment they keep it unto themselves, they would cease to prosper."

Happily, the women-folk of the Mathura's brahmins returned to the venue and told their husbands about the boon they had been blessed with. The male brahmins beat their head in disgust: "We are fools, who couldn't recognise the Lord Supreme playing so close to us! We had even maltreated their messenger. Rightly he has said that we are stupids and our ladies are really intelligent. We have lost a great opportunity. We now, thank you (the ladies) all for having ensured our prosperity, to some extent by your foresight and affectionate behaviour. We all are stupid!" And it is claimed, that the boon still shows its effect upon a particular community of the brahmins hailing from Mathura.

# 27

# The Emancipation of Vidyadhara Sudarshana

It was the festival of Shivratri and Nanda Baba along with Krishna Balarama and Gops, left in their chariot to reach 'Amlakavana' to worship Lord Shiva. Reaching there, all took bath in the river close by. Then very ritually, they kept the fast to propitiate Lord Shiva and Mother Goddess and gave alms to brahmans after feeding their cattle. But since their fast was to continue for the entire night, Nanda Baba and seniors partook of only little water.

While Nanda Baba was sitting before the emblem of Lord Shiva, there appeared a massive python searching for its prey, as it was very hungry. He found Nanda Baba's extended foot to be a convenient target and swallowed it. Nanda Baba yelled: "O Krishna! O Balarama! Come here. A python is swallowing me. Come to my rescue." Hearing the voice of Nanda Baba, Balarama, and other Gops reached near him with various sticks and stones in their hands. Krishna was a little far away so he took some time. But no matter how severely Balarama and other Gops beat the python, it didn't let go off Nanda Baba's leg. Nanda Baba was crying in pain. Then arrived Krishna and as he touched the python's body, it not only released Nanda Baba but also transformed its appearance. In a moment, all found that instead of the python, there stood a handsome man. He told that his name was Sudarshan Vidyadhara. In his earlier life, he was a rich person with a good physique. This made him naughty and arrogant. Once, when he was flying in his Vimana, he found the students of the grand sage Angira's hermitage loitering beneath. Seeing them, he had mocked at their ugliness. This was enough to infuriate the sage who cursed him: "Now fall down to the earth in the form of a deadly python."

Whereupon Sudarshan Vidyadhara requested the sage to dilute the curse. The sage said: "It won't be diluted. But in the Dwapar Yug, when Krishna touches your body, you shall be released from this curse."

Concluding this Sudarshana Vidyadhara said: "I am grateful to that great sage, since his curse gave me an opportunity to behold the Lord's form." Then he returned to his assigned realm, praising the Lord and singing his glory. The Vrajavasi happily returned to Gokula, completing Lord Shiva's worship at the expiry of the night.

□□

# 28

# Akroora's Confusion Dispelled

When Akroora was sent by Kansa to bring Krishna and Balarama to Mathura, Akroora was thrilled. He had immense love for the Vraja-kshetra and he knew that Lord Hari had incarnated as Krishna in this very area. He was delighted to get an opportunity to visit the holy place and take the Lord along with him. It was an occasion for him to rejoice, since he was a devotee of Lord Hari.

As he reached close to Nanda's village, he met Krishna and Balarama on the way playing with their friends. Although they were hardly 10-11 years old, they appeared to be very powerful and handsome. Akroor was ecstatic on seeing the Lord in a child's form. The Lord lovingly touched his feet alongwith his brother and friends and Akroora felt quite embarrassed. "Lord! Let me touch your feet, as you are the succour of this entire universe." he said in his mind.

Gradually the chariot guided by the Gops, reached Nanda's place. Nanda welcomed Akroora and asked about his welfare. Akroora said: "People of Mathura are longing to see your brave sons. Their maternal uncle, Kansa has sent an invitation to them, to attend the function to be held in Mathura. I am here to take them to Mathura."

Soon the news spread, that Akroora had come to take Krishna and Balarama to Mathura. Getting it, the entire village thronged at Nanda's place, violently protesting against Krishna and Balarama's departure to Mathura. The Gops rushed to Mother Yashoda, chanting their beloved Kanha's name and weeping bitterly. Yashoda herself was a picture of grief. How could she allow her 'Lalla' to go to Mathura? How she could have tolerated this separation from her beloved son? But calmly pacifying all of them Krishna said: "Don't worry. Let me finish the job, I have been waiting to accomplish. Soon I shall be back." With this promise, he sat on the seat in the chariot. It left for Mathura, with him, Akroora and Balarama seated in it.

After travelling for a while, they reached the bank of Yamuna. Akroora desired to have his bath there. So leaving Krishna and Balarama in the chariot, he went to the water and took a dip. As he went beneath the water surface, he felt as if Krishna and Balarama, in their most brilliant form, were also inside the water. Quickly he emerged out of the water to look towards his chariot. But both the brothers were very much present in it. He again took a dip and lo behold, the Lord Hari was seen lying on the coil of the serpent face who resembled Balarama. Lord Hari also appeared to be the true image of Lord Krishna. Bewildered, he again came out of the water and saw towards his chariot. He was surprised to see that Krishna and Balarama, both were sitting quietly on the chariot. Seeing his amazed face, Lord Krishna asked him: "Why do you look so perplexed ? Did you see anything strange in the Yamuna waters?" When Akroora looked at the two brothers, he again saw their same images.

Then closing his eyes, he prayed: "O Lord! Don't confuse me further. I know now who you two really are!" Whereupon the two brothers displayed their celestial form to Akroora and touched his head. As they touched him, his confusion vanished. "I see now Lord, you control every bit of Creation. Thus far I was under the impression as if your incarnation was confined to your person only. Victory of the Lord Hari!" Saying so, Akroora fell at Krishna's feet. Raising him up and pressing him to his heart, Krishna said: "Now take us to Mathura to destroy its tyrant ruler. I have incarnated myself on the earth to rid of his all fears." And then he took them to Mathura.

☐☐

# 29

# Krishna And Kubja

As soon as the chariot carrying Akroora, Krishna and Balarama reached close to Mathura, both the brothers got down from it, with the promise to meet him at the court of Kansa next day morning and joined their friends who had arrived to a picnic spot at the periphery of Mathura.

After refreshing themselves Krishna and Balarama set out with their Gop friends to see the city of Mathura. It was gaiety decorated with much crowd, enthusiastically welcoming the wrestlers from outside, who had come there to participate in the wrestling competition. However, seeing these two youth from Nandgram, they were captivated. All men, women, older and young rushed to behold them. Krishna and Balarama were moving on the streets of Mathura in a gay-caviller fashion. On their way, they happened to meet a washerman. Seeing him carrying a bundle of royal clothes, freshly washed and pressed for the king, they asked him to give some of the clothes from the bundle to their friends, who were not so well dressed. When that royal servant refused, they forcibly snatched the bundle and distributed the clothes to their friends and also to the onlookers. The washerman rushed to Kansa to report the matter to him.

Then the group from Nandagram happened to spot a tailor. They forced him to adjust the clothes, as much, to make them suit their bodies. Krishna was behaving as if he had every right upon his maternal uncle's property. Wearing a new set of clothes, the group moved on.

Krishna spotted a beautiful woman coming with perfumes and lotions and going towards the royal place. Krishna took the plate from her. She was also captivated by Krishna's charm. While she looked at him with a bewitching smile, Krishna pressed down her feet by implanting his feet upon them and gave a powerful thrust to his neck from the point of the chin. Lo and behold! The hump was gone in a trice. There stood a comely, well-endowed woman with a flawless body. Out of sheer gratitude, she requested Krishna to follow her to her house where she wanted to treat him well. But Krishna said: "No, Kubja! I have some other important appointment at present, accomplishing which, I shall surely come to your place." Then they (Balarama, Krishna and Gops) moved on and getting guided by the local people, they reached close to the venue of the competition. As they were about to enter it, Kansa, who had been getting the every minute reports of their pranks, instructed his mahout to let loose his mad elephant, Kuwaliya peeda, on to the boys. But undaunted, they killed the elephant in no time, and each of them plucking one tusk of the elephant, quite heroically and triumphantly reached the venue. Their message to Kansa was clear: "We can't be frightened with the show of naked, animal force. Now we have come prepared for the decisive battle."

And the next day, they put the tyrant ruler to death.

□□

# 30

# Krishna Meets His Parents For The First Time

Following the slaying of Kansa, Krishna and Balarama rushed to the royal prison where their (real) parents were anguishing for about a decade and half. They opened the chains-locks themselves and released their parents. Both Vasudeva and Devaki had their throats choking in the excessive emotion, for they never expected the release and meeting with their sons as they knew the might of the tyrant ruler Kansa. Little they could imagine, that their sons were the mighty Masters of the entire universe. While one of them provided support to the earth to make it stay on an even keel, the other ensured the existence of the rightous order over it. Father Vasudeva pressed them to his heart, when they bowed to touch his feet. Mother Devaki looked bewildered and dazed in her stream of emotions passing through her heart. The unfortunate woman, who, though begot eight issues, could not see even the face of any one of them. Both the boys clung to her bosom as if they were still infants. Words, then appeared too weak a medium to convey their feelings truthfully.

At last, regaining his composure, Krishna said: "O Sire! Pardon us for the delay in ensuring your release."

| | | |
|---|---|---|
| **Vasudeva** | : | "Pardon! I never expected it." |
| **Devaki** | : | "Where is Kansa!" |
| **Balarama** | : | "We have already killed him!" |
| **Devaki** | : | "Killed? But you both are only lads, and he was quite powerful." |
| **Vasudeva** | : | "Oh really! Well done my boys!" |
| **Devaki** | : | "But Krishna, remember that he was your maternal Uncle. See to it that his funeral is performed properly." |

Assuring her of it, both the boys took out their parents and leading a huge procession, took them round the city. The people of the city were rejoicing and welcoming the procession, while chanting: "Chhacha ke pivaiyya ne chhatrapati maro hai" [He whose stable diet was only whey has managed to slay an overlord].

Taking their parents to a palace made for them and ensuring all comforts to them, Krishna and Balarama went to set free the arrested king of Mathura, Ugrasen, the father of Kansa. Then through a formal ceremony, the king was restored to the throne. Having made the arrangement for the funeral of Kansa, Krishna and Balarama returned to Nanda Baba, who was camping on the outskirts of Mathura.

"Baba! Now you can fearlessly return to village! For, we will have to stay here for a few more days."

Nanda Baba who was stunned said, "No-No....... You must come back to village with us. After all, we all have some right over you."

Reassuring him, Krishna said: "No doubt you and Ma Yashoda are our real parents and you have every right over us. But we have to first set the order right. We will soon come back".

And then both the lads tearfully bade farewell to Nanda Baba. As Nanda reached home, Yashoda questioned him for his returning alone. "How could you have such a hard heart to leave our kids there?"

Then Nanda Baba told her all that happened in Mathura: "Kanha promised me that soon he will return home with Balarama."

When the Gops heard about their Kanha's extended stay in Mathura, they dashed their heads in an uncontrollable agony. Since then, they kept on wishing for their Kanha's return. Meanwhile, Mathura was resounding with joyful songs, while Vraja was sorrowing for the absence of Kanha.

❑❑

# 31

## Jarasandha Attacks Mathura

Jarasandha, the powerful and tyrant ruler of Magadha, was the father-in-law of Kansa. He had his two daughters married to Kansa. After their husband's death, the daughters, named Arti and Prapti, went to stay with their father. Jarasandha was shocked to know about Kansa's death. At once, he decided to exterminate the Yadava family. With this intention, he gathered a huge army and surrounded Mathura. He had many powerful Asuras with him.

Krishna took it as a good opportunity to slay the rogues in one go, for that was the very purpose of his incarnation. As he thought of slaying the evil persons, his bow, mace, the Chakra Sudarshana all came automatically in his hands. Balrama was also ready with his army, armed with clubs and ploughs. When Jarasandha faced them, he shouted–"I shall not fight a duel with Krishna, the slayer of his maternal uncle. However, for me that match could be, robust Balarama."

Srikrishna contemptuously told him: "The brave don't use words to show their prowess in a war but weapons. Take up your arms."

And then a fierce battle ensued. Krishna-Balarama made an enhancement of Jarasandha's huge army. Balarama not only captured Jarasandha but tying his hands and feet, threw him in a bundle-form before Krishna. Krishna pardoned him, with the thought that his collecting the huge army of the evil persons and attacking Mathura would help him in exterminating the evil loads on the earth, without making any attempt to search and kill them individually.

Jarasandha returned to his capital severely trounced. But this did discourage him from collecting the army and attacking Mathura Though he attacked Mathura for 17 times, he was defeated every ti.

It was his 18th attack on Mathura, in which he came amassing a v.

huge army. He was also joined by Kalyavana with his 30 million strong forces, who was duped into coming in the open, to fight against Krishna by the sage Narada.

Meanwhile, hearing that the enemy forces were marching toward Mathura, Krishna and Balarama also chalked out their strategy. In order to divert the enemy the two brothers had a secret fort built, surrounded by the ocean on the western coast with the help of the divine architect Vishwakarma. The fort was made so strong that even air couldn't have passed through it without Krishna's order. They called it Dwarikapuri. And in no time, they shifted most of their clan people to it. Indra had also contributed by donating his Sudharma Hall, which was created with such fineness that hunger, thirst and unrighteousness could n't have entered it.

Having made these preparations, Krishna with Balarama left Mathura through its main gate, armed with their divine weapons.

Kalyavana, who had already surrounded Mathura, saw a grand person, well armed, leaving the city. He came chasing him, who was no one else but Krishna himself and entangling Kalayavana was a part of his strategy. Krishna also pretended, as though he was fleeing the city in panic. Now Kalyavana was trailing him, challenging him, "O Coward! Stay there! It is not feat for the brave to flee the battle field." Although this act earned an epithet for Krishna, Ranachoddas, Krishna didn't stop. While moving ahead, he spotted a deep cave and quietly entered into it. In that cage was asleep Muchukunda, a powerful king of the Ikshavaaku Dynasty. He had done a long penance and had also rendered much help to the gods. The Gods, then asked him to seek any boon in return, save the boon of Moksha- the final salvation of the soul. Whereupon the king Muchukund, tired of travelling, had asked the boon of undisturbed sleep for a long duration. The Gods granted the boon and promised : "Whosoever you see first, after your sleep is disturbed, shall be incinerated by your fiery gaze, almost instantly."

Krishna knew about his this boon and the presence of the king inside that cave. As he reached the cave, Krishna quietly covered the sleeping body with his distinct yellow covering raiment called Pitamber. So, when chasing Krishna the demon Kalayavana entered the cave, he thought Krishna himself was having a nap, covering himself with his Pitamber. As he woke up the sleeping figure who was actually Raja Muchukunda, the king cast his fiery gaze upon Kalyavana, who was instantly burnt to ashes by virtues of the boon that the king had.

This way, ensuring Kalyavana's end, Krishna appeared before King Muchukunda and having granted him his Darshana, allowed the king to get a place in his Vaikuntha.

Then he came out and wiped off Kalayavana's leader-less army in no time. Upon returning to Mathura, he took possession of all the wealth that Kalayavana had and made preparation to go back finally to Dwarika. Meanwhile, Jarasandha launched his 18th attack on Mathura. Krishna pretended to be fleeing in panic and managed to force Jarasandha to go toward the western coast. There Jarasandha couldn't spot him, he set fire on the entire mountain and returned helplessly, as there was no one against whom be could have fought. Thus, having misled Jarasandha, Krishna quietly jumped from the mountain into the ocean and reached the safety of his Dwarika fort. Balarama also reached there, when Jarasandha returned to Magadha.

Much later, Krishna devised a plan before the Pandva's performance of the Rajasooya Yagya, to take along Arjuna and Bhima to Magadha and to have Jarasandha torn to death in an open wrestling but Krishna knew that Jarasandha was born with his body divided into two different parts. It was the maid Jara, who made the two parts joint together. So Krishna knew Jarasandha's physical weakness. He hinted at Bhima to tear him into two pieces. This was how, Krishna eventually got rid of his deadly enemy, the tyrant ruler, Jarasandha.

◻◻

# 32

## Krishna Sends Uddhava To Vraja

Much before Jarasandha episode, when Krishna was still based in Mathura, one day he called his dear friend Uddhava and asked him to go to Vraja (Nandagram Barsana. Gokul etc.) and report the welfare of his Nanda Baba, Mother Yashodha and the dear Gopis.

Uddhava was a learned man. He believed in the Inpresonal form of God, though he knew that Krishna was an incarnation of the Supreme Spirit. He also claimed to be the top devotee of Lord Krishna but said that one should worship the Formless Supreme and not His Manifest Form. It was also to teach Uddhava a lesson, in realising as to what the real love was, that Krishna sent him to Vraja.

Uddhava left early in morning to reach Nandagrama at the evening. When Nanda Baba saw him, the bosom friend of his beloved Kanhaiya, he came forward to welcome him. Uddhava resembled Krishna so much that Nanda Baba felt as though he was embracing his beloved Kanhaiya only.

After making him rest for a while, both of them sat to have food. "Uddhava! Now that my friend Vasudeva and his wife Devaki are out of the prison, his family must be heaving a sigh of relief. Also, now they have their sons with them." Nanda Baba said.

"But both Krishna and Balarama," Uddhava said, "particularly Krishna still belong to this palce. He misses you all and his childhood friends, very badly. Since he is too busy in resetting the rule of Mathura, he sent me to learn about your welfare and give the message, that as soon as he is free he will be back here."

This message cheered Nanda and Yashoda a bit. Soon the word spread that Kanha had made his dear friend come to reassure all, that he would soon be here. All the Gops and Gopis rushed to the place.

Seeing their totally self-less and untained love for Krishna, Uddhava was little surprised. "So intense a love with no desire in return? Even we, the worshipper of the Formless God, desire at least our salvation through the worship! But what do they love for? just a benign look from their beloved Kanha and nothing else?" Even while thinking this way, he thought they ought to be initiated in the Formless worship so that they realised the impermanence of the mortal relations.

"Yes, your Kanha would come", began Uddhava, "But you should know that nothing is permanent in this mortal world. You won't get solace if you remain infatuated to mortal persons. Concentrate better on the Impersonal (Nirgun) Form, which may provide salvation to your souls."

This was countered by those illiterate Gops with very strong arguments. Since they felt shy in talking to a man so openly, they chose a flower-bee moving around there, to address. Though they directed all their pleas and arguments to Uddhava[1]. The gopis treated the Impersonal God with scant contempt. They maintained that it was not the question of choosing the better God; for their simple heart knew no reason for love. "That we love Kanha, is beyond logic. Now we can't change it. Morever if you like bitter plumes, no matter how sweet the mangoes be, you will not prefer them over your natural choice. Hence don't waste your arguments on us, as we are eternally Kanha's. He is our immutable and final choice till we are conscious of our existence."

Uddhava had nothing, to counter these feelingful pleas. But, nevertheless, he found that region to be so captivating that he kept on staying there for days, although he had to return soon. The guileless love of the people, also had bound Uddhava with their affection.

Then at last, one day, bidding alieu to all of them with a heavy heart and carrying various gifts for 'Kanha', he left for Mathura.

As he reached before Krishna, he told him all about his visit and the strange experience of pristine love. "Really Lord," Uddhava told Krishna in private, "Now I realise your uncontrollable yearning for that area. Their love is so pristine and pure that you feel just helpless before it. You forget all about temporariness and eternity, the tangible and intangible and feel rejuvenated in that love every moment."

Whereupon, a visibly distressed Krishna said with tearful eyes: "Uddhava! That's why I can't forget my Vraja and my people. They have no parallel in this world or any other. I am inseparable from them and so shall I ever be."

◻◻

---

There are many top class lyrical poems written by Uddhava not only in Sanskrit but in Hindi which are called in general, the 'Bee-Lyrics' or 'Bhramar-Geet'.

# 33

## Krishna Marries Rukmini

The ruler of the kingdom of Vidarbha, Raja Bheeshmaka had five sons and one beautiful daughter called Rukmini. The name of his eldest son was Rukmi, while the names of the younger ones were Rukmaratha, Rukmabahu, Rukmkisha and Rukmali. Rukmini was, in fact, the incarnation of Goddess Lakshmi. When she heard from the bards, about the qualities, beauty and bravery of Krishna, she mentally decided to marry him only. Krishna had also developed liking for her, having heard from people about Rukmini's incomparable charms and abilities. However, her brother Rukmi was jealous of Krishna since he preferred Shishupal. He wanted Rukmini to be married off to Shishupal. Though Shishupal was Krishna's brother, since Shishupal's mother was a cousin of Vasudeva, right since his childhood, he had developed enmity for Krishna owing to his inferiority complex as he could never match Krishna in any field.

Rukmini was perturbed knowing about Rukmi's intentions. One day she called her trusted priest, a brahmina, and secretly asked him to go to Dwarika and tell Krishna about her love for him. "Tell him that I won't marry anyone else but him, while my brother is forcing me to marry Shishupal. So there is not much time for him if he cares to honour my love for him."

The brahmin quietly left for Dawarika and reaching there delivered the message, that Rukmini had sent specially to Lord Krishna. Krishna was mentally disturbed getting this request. "My beloved should not be put to any problem, till I am here". And he asked his charioteer to ready the vehicle for his departure to a far off place, Kundanipur, the capital of Vidharbha. He took along the brahmin also, to guide the way. He travelled non stop to reach there in time. He remembered that Rukmini had hinted her readiness to get away in his company. She had conveyed: "A day prior to marriage, it is customary for the daughters to go to the hill, having Goddess

Girija's temple and seek her blessings, for getting the husband of their choice." The brahmina had also told the possible date of Rukmini's proposal. Hence he travelled so fast.

The marriage was scheduled to take palce on the following day. In fact the 'Barat' of Shishupal was already in town as Rukmi was not prepared to take any chances against that 'mayavee' [deft in duping people] Krishna. Shishupal had many friends, who were sworn enemies of Krishna and Balaram. They had recieved the report from their sleuths about Kirshna's leaving for some 'unknown destination' and Balaram following him soon after.

Balaram followed Krishna to Kundanipur, sensing the danger involved, in Krishna going alone to elope with a willing Rukmini. Shishupal was to reach there with full funfare with large groups of the mighty kings like Jarasandha etc., who had been his close friend particularly because he belonged to the anti-Krishna group.

As the appointed day approached, Rukmini was worried. "Could that brahmina deliver my message to my chosen Lord? Has the Lord himself refused to come? What should I do?"

As if God listened to her, there appeared, suddenly, a tired but beaming brahmina, Rukmini was waiting for–with a acceptable nod to convey that the job had been accomplished. Then brahmina privately told her that Krishna would wait at the point where the way from the temple reached the planes, in his chariot.

Rukmini was thrilled. Her dream was becoming a reality. Hastily she took a bath, donned fresh robes to join her waiting friends with the plates full with lighted lamps and auspicious things for the worship of the Goddess in their hands. Singing an auspicious song, they left for the temple.

Rukmini completed the worship with a buoyant heart: "Bless me to become Krishna's wife!" she prayed quietly. As she did, a solitary flower fell from the idol over Rukmini's bowed head, to convey the Goddess's blessings.

Now cautiously Rukmini began to return, casting her eyes everywhere, very slowly. As the group reached the plain level, she found her dream man standing there with his chariot ready. Though Rukmini saw him for the first time in reality, she could recognise Krishna. A darkish complexion, the shoulders draped in a yellow garment, the crown of the peacock feather adorning his head. She rushed towards the waiting chariot.

Krishna helped her mount the chariot and in no time, they were almost flying away followed by the aghast soldiers of the king. As the matter was reported, many kings led by the 'bridegroom' Shishupal, rushed to 'rescue' Rukmini from Krishna's arms, little realising, that she was herself helping Krishna to take her away.

But that time Balarama had also reached there with his army. A feirce battle ensued there. Krishna and Balarama created such a havoc as to force all friends of Shishupal, including Jarasandh to flee. In no time, the Yadu-dynasty's army won the battle with all Shishupal's friends and Shishupal himself, running away.

They reached Rukmi to tell him about his sister's elopement with Krishna. Rukmi was angry. He said, "I now depart with my army to teach these Gwalas a lesson. I take a vow, that I shall not return to the capital till I have rescued my sister from Krishna's fold."

In no time, he reached close to the Yadava Army and the battle began again. But while Balarama checked the rest of the enemy's army, Krishna took on Rukmi. He defeated him so thorough that Krishna could have easily hacked off his head. But Rukmini prayed him to let her brother return. But Krishna said: "He needs to be taught a lesson." He disfugured Rukmi by shaving off his eye-brows, moustaches, beard in a peculiar way and tied his hands and feet with his Pitamber. At last Balarama requested Krishna to let Rukmi return alive. "Insulting this way a noble is tantamount to killing him. Now, even otherwise, he is your brother-in-law."

Rukmi returned, beaten and insulted but he didn't enter his capital, following his vow. He established a small town called Bhojapur, close to Kundanipur.

Subsequnetly, Rukmi was killed, when in a gambling bout he tried to cheat Balarama. It happened on the occasion of Rukmi's grand daughter Rochana's marriage to Lord Krishna and Rukmini's grandson, Pradyumna's son, Aniruddha, when provoked by his friends Rukmi invited Balarama to a gambling session. Although Balarama was not a deft dicer, yet he was favoured by luck and went on winning the stapes. This made Rukmi, indulge in unfair means and despite a heavenly voice's warning him, he kept on cheating Balarama, who at last couldn't put up with the dishonesty of Rukmi and broke his head with a club.

□□

## 34

# Kamdeva Regains His Body in the Form of Pradyumna

We all know that in the attempt to disturb Lord Shiv's concentration, Kamadeva, the Lord of love, had his body incinerated, by the fiery gaze cast on him by the Lord. Kama's wife, Rati was all grief-stricken, knowing about her husband's untimely demise. When she prayed the Lord, Shankar assured her: "He has lost his body and not the spirit. And he would regain his body when he is born in Dwapar as Lord Krishna's son, Pradyumna. In the meantime, you should wait at demon Shambar's palace because it is there that you will meet your lost husband." Rati had no go but to stay at that demon's palace, in the form of a maid servant.

When Krishna married Rukmini, their eldest son was Pradyumna and an exact copy of the physically exterminated Kamadeva. He also resembled a lot with his father.

While the son was not even 10 days old, he was stolen by Shambharasura and was thrown into the ocean to settle his old score against Krishna. When the infant was tossed up into the ocean, he was swallowed by a fish, who itself was swallowed by an alligator. A fisherman happened to net that alligator and when he slit its belly open, he found a small but extremely charming human infant. The (maid) Rati was also present there and she was amazed to notice the similarity in the features of that boy and her husband, Kamadeva. She managed to get the boy for rearing up from that fisherman, who had no objection.

Once the divine sage Narud happened to reach there and he further confirmed: "He is no one else but Kamadeva, your husband. Now he has taken birth in the dynasty of Yadu, as Krishna's son."

Soon the boy became adolescent. His incomparable beauty often made Rati look at the boy as her husband. Once reading her expressions even Pradyumna asked: "Why there is a streak, in your look, of amorousness, when you are my mother?" Then Rati, who adopted a name Mayawati in this role, told him frankly: "You are not my son but huaband." Rati also gave him instructions in all the wonderous arts and sciences that she knew including the Mohini Vidya [The art of captivating others]. One day she told him that, when he (Pradyumna) was just ten days old, the demon Shambar had stolen him. "You are, actually, the son of Krishna and Rukmini." Pradyumna, then insisted on knowing about the entire episode and Rati obliged.

Armed with the secret tricks of capturing the opponent, Pradyumna came out to challange Shambar for a duel. The demon came out with his deadly mace, which he cast on Pradyumna who very casually warded it off. Then he used the special knowledge, he had acquired from Mayawati and killed the demon. Subsequently, on his request Mayawati took Pradyumna to Dwariaka through the aerial route. Seeing the couple [Pradyumna and Mayawati or Kamadev and Rati] the sentinels guarding the gate were confused thoroughly. They thought as if Krishna and Rukmini had come there. When the information was given inside, all the prominent members of the Yadu clan reached there, including Krishna, Balarama, Vasudeva and others. The seniors accepted the couple after lavishly blessing them. The family got back its lost son and Rati her lost husband. Dawarikapuri celebrated the occasion with great fan-fare and festivity.

❏❏

# 35

# The Syamantak Mani (Gem) Episode

One of the stalwarts of the Yadava clan in Dawarika, was Satyajit. He was an ardent worshipper of Lord Sun. Propitiated by his worship, the Lord appeared before him and granted to him a gem called Syamantak. The gem radiated with such a dazzling light that the people of Dwarika thought, as though Lord Sun had given to Satyajit, his own radiance. That gem used to give about 8 'bhara' (nearly 80 tolas) gold every day. Lord Krishna said that the gem must be deposited in the royal treasury but Satyajit refused.

One day Satyajit's brother, Prasenjit, had gone for hunting with that gem on his person. But unfortunately, he was devoured by a lion. When Prasen failed to return, Satyajit blamed Krishna for plotting the murder of his brother for the sake of usurping that gem. Since Krishna had some reservation about Satyajit's family retaining the properietorship of that gem, purely for security seasons though, people discerned some truth in Satyajit's blame.

Now Krishna had to prove his innocence. So taking clue from Prasenjit's friends, Krishna left to recover the gem. Meanwhile, the lion, who devoured Prasenjit happened to reach near a cave in which the bear Jambavant-of Ramayana fame was staying with his family. Jambavanta happened to kill that lion. He happened to find the gem inside the lion's body, since its radiance was sparkling even from outside of the lion. Having killed the lion, he gave that gem to his daughter, Jambavati.

One day, when Jambavati was playing with that gem, Krishna happened to reach close to her and recognised the gem by its brilliance. When he tried to snatch that gem from Jambvati, she yelled for her father, Jambavant's support who came and then a fierce battle ensued between the bear and Krishna which lasted for many days. At last, Jambavanta realised his fighting against his chosen Lord Ram in a different form. He apologized for his enmity and sought Krishna's forgiveness. In return, he gave the gem to Krishna and also made his daughter marry Krishna. Krishna returned triumphantly with the gem and yet another bride for him. Having proved his innocence this way, Krishna gave that gem back to Satyajit, while saying: "It is for its security reasons, that I wanted it deposited in the royal treasury." But Satyajit promised to pay the gold yielded by the gem, everyday to the royal treasury while desiring to retain the ownership of the gem. It was mutually agreed. In order to get over his guilty conscience on account of his falsely blaming Krishna for the theft, he also requested Krishna to accept his daughter, Satyabhama, as wife. Krishna agreed. But the troubles due to that gem, were far from over.

Coveting for that gem, were many in that Yadava clan. Once, when Krishna-Balarama were out of Dwarika, having gone to Hastinapur to enquire about their Bua (Father's Sister), Kunti's sons, the Pandavas, who were being distressed by their cousins, the Kauravas, Kritavarma and Akroora provoked Shatadhanva, yet another chieftain of the Yadavs against Satyajit. They told him: "Satyabhama was to be married to you. Now having fallen under Krishna's influence, Satyajit got her married to Krishna. This is a direct insult to you." Their game was polluting Shatadhanwa's mind, as much against Satyajit, as to force him kill Satyajit so that the gem could be snatched by them. Seizing his opportunity, Shatadhanwa went in a furious mood to Satyajit and killed him. He stole the gem from the deadman's body and returned to Dwarika safely.

Learning about Shatadhanwa's killing her father, Satyabhama was shocked. But she couldn't have done much since Krishna was not in Dwarika. With the result, she rushed to Hastinapur and told Krishna and Balaram about all that transpired in Dwarika in their absence. Both the brothers returned and began to search for Shatadhanwa.

Meanwhile, in Dwarika, Shatadhanwa could not get the support of either Kritavarma or Akroora, who feared Krishna's retaliation since they knew that Krishna was returning to Dwarika. Hence, in order to play safe, they refused to help Shatadhanwa. On the contrary, they expelled him from their palace.

Shatadhanwa was now isolated. He started to run coastwards to escape Krishna's wrath. But Krishna was in his hot pursuit. In no time, he caught hold of Shatadhanwa and had him beheaded with his Chakra Sudarshana. Then he searched for the Syamantaka Mani before returning to Dwarika. But he couldn't find it. It was not with Shatadhanwa. Akroora had already usurped that gem before having him expelled from his palace.

Though Krishna returned without the gem, he was sure that the gem was still in Dwarika. It was confirmed by his sleuths. He knew that the gem was too brilliant to be hidden. Soon it was detected on the person of Akroora, who of late, had started looking very brilliant. One day Krishna called him and said in private: "Uncle! We don't want that gem. You may retain it. But what I want is that you must display it before Dauoo and others so that they could feel reassured that gem is still in Dwarika."

Akroora eventually agreed. After displaying the gem in the court, Krishna allowed Akroora to keep possession of it. But that gem proved inauspicious for the Yadava clan, as soon after, the Yadavs perished fighting each other.

◻◻

# 36

## Shalva Attacks Dwarika

One of Shishupal's bosom friend was Raja Shalva. He was in the group of the kings who had gone with Shishupal to Kundanipur to ensure that his friend married Rukmini. But when she chose to elope with Krishna, Shalva decided to exterminate the whole of the Yadav clan. With this intention he started worshipping Mahadeva. The Great Lord Shiv appeared before Shalva to bless him. The King demanded from the Lord, a Vimana (an air vehicle) which might be unassailabe for any one–Gods, men, naga, gandharva, kinnar and that might reach the desired destination, merely by his wishing for it. Shiv said 'so be it' and returned to Kailash. Following his order the demons' architect, Mayadanava quickly prepared the desired vehicle for Shalva. By that time Shishupal had been slain by Lord Krishna, which made this king all the more angry. Sitting in his wonderous vehicle, he launched an attack on Dwarika.

Krishna and Baralrma, at that time, were in the Pandavas' newly created capital called Indraprastha. With the result, the responsibility of protecting Dwarika fell on Kritaverma, Akroora, Samba and other Yadava stalwarts. But they could not stand before Shalva's ferocious attack, who was also deft in casting illusions with the help of his expertise in black magic. He enveloped whole of the battle field with darkness at the noon, to the great distress of the Yadava Army. At last using his fiery arrows, Pradyumna managed to dispelled that sham darknes. This charged Shalva's minister, Dhymaan to attack Pradyumna with a deadly mace, which torn in twain, Pradyumna's bosom. Deeming him dead, though he was only unconscious, his charioteer drove him to the safety of Dwarika. Getting well, he returned soon to the battle field and kept on fighting Shalva for 27 days.

Meanwhile, Krishna in Indraprastha was visualising pronouncedly ominous indications. He told his brother Balarama: " I think that all is not well in Dwarika and we must return." And bidding adieu to the Pandavas and their Bua, Kunti, the two brothers reached Dwarika. Krishna made his brother look after the security of Dwarika and he himself went straight to the battle field.

As the Yadava army heard the unmistakable resounding blow of the conch-shell 'Panchajanya', they felt reassured realising that their leader was there to help them.

Seeing Krishna entering the battle field, Shalva cast his deadly weapon, aiming at Krishna's charioteer. But Krishna managed to cut it mid way by his disc. Then he hurled so many arrows by his famous 'Sharnga' bow, that Shalva was greatly distressed. He immediately disappeared using his maya-power, to Krishna's great surprise. While he was searching for Shalva, Krishna saw weeping brahmina giving him the message: "Shalva had kidnapped Vasudeva Ji. Come to rescue him quickly." Krishna was taken aback a bit but soon regained his composure, thinking : "How that rogue could have entered Dawrika guarded by Dauoo? It is all illusion." Then he spotted Shalva again in his Vimana. This time Krishna threw his mace Kaumudki, aiming at him, which reduced the vehicle to pieces. Shalva fell on to the ground. Then, since he was out of his vehicle, Krishna easily beheaded him with his disc Sudarshana. As he killed Shalva, a divine light emerged from the dead king's body and coalesced with the radiance of Krishna's body. At that time Shalva's one friend Dantavakra also attacked. Krishna killed him also by his one mace blow. Shalva's yet other brother Vidur was also killed in this battle. Salva's death considerably lessened the burden of the earth as he was also a rogue.

◻◻

# 37

# Krishna Behead Shishupal

That Krishna had a special affection for the Pandavas, is a well known fact. When the Pandavas, having secured half of the kingdom of Hastinapur as their due share by the consent of the Kuru Dynasty's seniors, decided to celebrate the occasion, they were advised to perform the famous 'Rajsooya Yagya' to establish their supremacy. For that, they made many elaborate preparations under Krishna's directions. They sent their representatives all around to procure huge wealth for the Yagya and invite the kings from all over the earth. They also established a separate capital for them, called Indraprastha, on the western bank of Yamuna. They were supported by Maya danava, who constructed a beautiful palace for them. This architect also got them many divine weapons. Although the Kauravas apparently agreed to help the Pandavas performing this Yagya, they were turning green with envy at the Pandavs' prosperity. It was to deprive the Pandavas of all this grandeur that the cunning Duryodhana had, later on, hatched the gamble conspiracy which eventually led to Pandava's defeat, their banishment and then finally led them to massive confrontation called Mahabharat.

However, these are all the subsequent events. At the time of performing the Rajsooya Yagya, under Krishna's advice, they managed to eliminate many tyrants including Jarasandha, though Shishupal managed to survive.

Shishupal was also Krishna's cousin from his mother's side. He always carried a grudge against Krishna. When Shishupal was only an infant, Krishna reached near his mother. Shishupal had an extra arm at the time of his birth and according to a divine prophesy, he in whose lap, the infant was to lose his extra arm, was to be the slayer of this body. And as Krishna took him in his lap, Shishupal lost his extra limb. This made his mother nervous and Krishna assured her: "I won't touch him till he commits 100 offenses against me. But as soon as he crosses this mark, I shall make the prophesy true."

When all preparations for the 'Rajsooya Yagya' had been completed, the question arose as to who should be the first to be worshipped in that grand gathering of the top kings of the earth. Though there were many contestants for this prime-slot, the grand sire Bheeshma advised his grandsons, that the most deserving one was Lord Krishna, the Supreme Lord. While all agreed and the ceremony had also started, Shishupal rose up with his objections. He yelled at Yuddhisthar: "O Dharmaraj! You are said to be very wise but I regret your choice for this mere Gwala for the Agra-Pooja. How could you choose him when there are so many top kings like Duryodhan and myself. He doesn't deserve to have been invited to this great royal show, as he is not even a petty king, let alone getting this honour." And then he started abusing Krishna before that august assembly. Although there were many who were not in the favour of Krishna getting this top position, they dared not say it openly. But they sided with Shishupal, who threatened to ruin the show if Krishna was to be worshipped first. Krishna kept quiet for most of the time but when Shishupal crossed the limit of the offenses, Krishna quietly summoned his disc and beheaded Shishupal before everybody. The Kings favouring Shishupal were frightened and then no trouble arose in the Yagya's performance. Despite having been reverenced by all in that august assembly, Krishna chose for himself the job of washing the feet of all those invited to that Yagya. That showed his true greatness; he developed no arrogance despite having been so honoured and lovingly washed the feet of the guests. The whole assembly shouted in one voice with the slogan: "Long live Lord Krishna!"

❑❑

# 38

## Krishna Kills Narakasura And Releases The Helpless Women

During his stay on the earth, Lord Hari in the incarnation of Lord Krishna had single-handedly slayed many demons, rogues and vile persons. One of them was Narakasura (also called Bhaumasura). He was a lecherous ruler. But he is said to be the earth's son. The Srimad Bhagwat claims, that once earth begged from the three Super Gods that she should be blessed with a robust son. He was Narakasura, who was so much powerful as to snatch away from Lord Varuna's possession, his famous canopy, the 'Kundals' (ear-rings) from the divine mother, Aditi and the Maniparvata from the divine mountain Sumeru. This ruler was a lecherous demon. He had the ability to change his form and elope with lonely damsels whom he would marry forcibly for the sake of pleasure only. Then those defiled women would be imprisoned in the royal dungeon. Once he assumed the form of an elephant and carried off the daughter of Vishwakarma and outraged her. He also captured the daughters of Gandharvas, Gods, men and the divine nymphs themselves and thus had more than 16,000 women in his palace.

When his tyranny crossed all limits, Krishna flew with his wife Satyabhama on his celebrated mount, Garuda, and attacked his palace. It was guarded by a deadly demon Murya with his entire family. Although the fort was very well secure, Krishna easily penetrated into it and slayed not only Murya and his entire family but also subsequently Narakasura. As he did so, the earth, disguised in the form of a woman, reached there with Narakasura's son Bhagdatta and requested Lord Krishna to make him the ruler, which the lord accepted.

Then arose the big problem of settling the issue of the helpless women, kept imprisoned in Narakasura's dungeons. They prayed Krishna: "Don't send us back to our husbands, brothers etc. As they might not keep us now. Now we have no place to go. Where can we live with honour?" Then the Supreme Lord said: "Don't worry! You shall all be my queens and lead an honourable life. I am here to accept you all as my wives."

The helpless women couldn't have hoped for anything better. The discarded and defiled women were willingly being accepted by the lord, the only succour to the helpless.

While returning to Dwarika, on Indra's request who was delighted to get back all the divine objects, Krishna visited heaven in the company of Satyabhama. Indra was forced to present the couple, the divine tree of Parijaat which Krishna planted in Dwarika, to the great delight of Satyabhama. Thus the lord rescued all the helpless women and accorded them a respectable status in society.

◻◻

# 39

## Krishna And Balarama Pay Their Guru's Fees

When both Krishna and Balarama had grown up, Vasudeva, their father respectfully took them to their family Guru, Gargacharya, and requested him: "Gurudeva! Now these boys are big enough to commence their education." Gargacharya took them under his guidance and taught the basics, after initiating them into chanting the holy Gayatri mantra. Lord Hari completed all the 'Sanskars' like any common boy of his age would do. When their primary education was over, the Guru asked Vasudeva to send them to the Gurukul (school) run by the learned sage Sandeepani in Ujjaiyani or Ujjain. Staying there, the boys completed their education in record time. They learnt all about the Vedas, Upanishads, holy scriptures, Meemansa (logic), Jurisprudence etc. soon as both of the yoga and state-craft. In all, they took barely 64 days to master all there was to learn. Having completed their education in all respect, both the boys went to their Guru, Sandeepani and requested him with full respect, "O Gurudeva! By your grace and guidance we have completed our education. Now we are about to depart to our native place. But before doing so, we want to repay your fees, as the scriptures claim that without giving the guru his due fees, no education shall be fruitful. So we request you to tell us as to how should we pay the 'Guru Dakshina'.

Sandeepani was delighted to learn about his young students sentiments. He also knew that these two boys were no ordinary boys but the incarnations of the Lord Hari and Lord Sheshnag. So he also knew that they could accomplish even the impossible job. He also consulted his wife and on her advice, said to his students : "If both of you could get back our dead-son, who was drowned in the sea on the Prabhas-Kshetra shores, we shall deem that you have paid your Guru-Dakshina."

"Very well, Guru Dev," the boys said and left for the sea-shore. While they were sitting on the sea-shore to contemplate upon their course of action, the personified form of the sea appeared before them hand-bound. "What are you thinking Lord sitting on the shore? Can I be of any help?"

"Yes, you can. You know, some time back our Guru Sandeepani's young son was drowned. We want him back." Krishna said.

"That boy is not with me. He had been taken by a demon named Panchjanya who dwells deep inside me on a small island."

Getting this clue, both of them entered into the sea and straight away attacked the demon's citadel. But though they searched the entire place, they could not find any evidence of their Guru's son's presence there. However, when they took on the demon, he confessed to having killed that boy, whose spirit was now with the death God, Dharmaraja. Whereupon, they killed the demon. The demon had a beautiful conchshell, which gave a typical note when the air was blown into it. It was called Paanchjanya since it was found at the island Panchjan. Krishna took the conch in his possession. Thence forward, it became his distinct companion which he never lost.

Then both the brothers reached straight to the realm of death. They immediately asked Dharmaraja, to revive their Guru's son back to life. He did so quickly and handed over that boy to Krishna and Balarama. Taking along that revived son of their Guru, they rushed back to Ujjaiyini.

Their Guru was filled with joy to get back his lost dead son. The wife of the Guru showered choicest blessings upon Krishna and Balarama. Having paid their Guru's fees, they asked their Guru: "Could we do any thing more to make you happy or fulfil your any other wish?"

Sandeepani replied: "What more can I wish, when the Lord of three realms is standing before me as my student. I am totally content and happy with you. I have no desire left.

And then bidding adieu to their Guru and his family, both returned to Mathura amidst the great ovation by the people of Mathura, who had already heard the wondrous doings of their young heroes.

□□

# 40

# Sudama And Krishna

Sudama became very friendly with Krishna when the two met at the sage Sandeepani's school at Ujjaiyini. This was a very famous 'gurukul' (school) at that time, where students from far off places used to come to get their education. Sudama was a son of poor brahmina, while Shri Krishna and Balarama were the sons of Nanda, a renowned chieftain having a huge stock of the cows. There, at the hermitage of Sandeepani Guru, Krishna developed great friendship with Sudama. They became so close that, wherever the Guru sent them they used to go together.

Once they were sent by the Guru to fetch some dry woods' pieces from the jungle. While they were still busy in the job, it started raining very heavily. They immediately took shelter upon a big tree since, apart from rain, they also feared the beast on their prowl. But even though the night had set in and it ceased to pour heavily, fearing the beasts, they couldn't return. Now both were hungry, apart from being frightened in that lonely jungle amidst pelting rain. Atop a sturdy branch covered with dense leaves, they were waiting when Krishna heard a 'munching' voice. "Are you eating something Sudama?" he questioned.

"Here are some beaten rice. It was tucked up in my commerbund by my mother when I left home. Now it is coming very handy. I didn't offer you because it is a snack of the lowly people and not for princes like you." Sudama explained.

But without caring for the reason Sudama hesitated to offer him the beaten rice, Krishhna quickly took away a handful from the lap of Sudama where they were kept. And merrily he started munching them.

"They taste better than even 'Makhan-Misri' (butter and sugar candy mixture). And he kept on eating, to the great delight of Sudama. Then Krishna said: "Remember Sudama, that class consciousness should never figure between two dear friends."

When they returned, they found the hermitage people greatly worrying for them. After completing their education at the due time, both the friends parted, each going to one's native place.

When Sudama reached home after getting the education, he couldn't find a suitable job. With the result, he had a hard time since a mere primary school teacher's job wasn't sufficient to feed two persons. Sudama was married now. But he was a very self respecting person and one day he left that job also since he couldn't compromise on principles. Now his wife found it very difficult to make the two ends meet. Once he heard from a passerby that Krishna had become the ruler of Dwarika. Since Sudama's wife had heard a lot about her husband and Krishna's friendship from Sudama himself, she impressed upon her husband to go and seek help from his bosom friend. "May be, out of pity Shri Krishna ends all our misery!" But Sudama was reluctant to go. He was against seeking any help from any body. "If it is our destiny, we may languish in poverty. But I don't want to be obliged by anyone, not even by my childhood friend." Sudama countered the suggestion.

"Okay! Don't say anything to him. But least go to him, if for nothing than for congratulating him for becoming Dwarika's lord."

At last Sudama agreed to go. When he was leaving, his wife tucked up a small bundle containing beaten-rice, "These will help you on your way through the lonely jungles."

After many days, when tired and dirty Sudama reached before Dwarika Gate, he amazed the sentinel by disclosing his identity. "I am an old friend of your lord. Go and tell him that Sudama has arrived here."

Though initially refusing to go into the palace, the guard relented seeing Sudama's dominance to meet his old friend.

As the guard announced Sudama's arrival to Lord Krishna, the latter was filled with joy and excitement. At once, he left his throne and came running to the gate. "Oh dear friend," he said embracing Sudama. "Why did you take so long to come to me? It is for ages that

I have been trying to search for you. You appear quite distressed."

Sudama said: "It's due to the exhaustion I suffered on the way, that I look so. I am happy, otherwise." His self-respect didn't allow him to tell his rich friend about his tale of woe.

But seeing his condition, Lord Krishna was really sorry. He wept uncontrollably. Then he treated Sudama very lavishly. From his own hands he washed his feet, made him take bath with scented water and also dressed him in fine clothes. He made him sleep on his royal bed. He fed him lovingly with the choicest food. He also searched out the bundle containing the beaten rice. In light banter he said: "So again you were willing to eat it, all by yourself. I know my 'bhabhi' must have sent it for me. You greedy fellow!"

All this while Sudama continued to feel embarrassed. He had no words to say. While enjoying all royal comforts and enjoying choicest dishes, he remembered his wife. "That poor lady! She must be surviving on beaten rice! But what should I do? Should I tell Krishna about my real condition? But I can never do this. I can't be a beggar, no matter how distressed I may be. If its is God's wish, then I can't help."

This way many days passed. One day Sudama requested his friend: "Krishna! It is time I should return. My wife must be worrying." With great reluctance Krishna agreed. While Sudama was returning he continued to carry guilt-complex. "What should I tell my wife? God knows, in what condition she might be."

As he reached home, he was unable to search his house. For where his hut should have been, a huge palatial house stood. Bewildered, while he was standing before it, his wife emerged adorned with gold ornaments from head to toe. "Why are you standing outside your house? Come in, it is ours! Your friend has answered your prayers."

Feeling deeply grateful to his friend, Sudama couldn't even say that he had made no such prayer. But he didn't know that his Krishna knows the secret of all hearts?

❏❏

# 41

# Yashoda and Krishna's Reunion

All the scriptures of Hindu (Sanatana Dharma) claim that taking the holy-dip at the Brahma Kunda Sarovar (Brahma Kunda Pond) at Kurukshetra, gives the aspirant much merit. Recounting a story from Lord Krishna's life, Shukadeva Ji said to Raja Parikshit. "O King! Once a great solar eclipse appeared prior to the era of Mahabharat. In order to take the holy dip not only the Yadavas from Dwarika led by Shri Krishna, Balarama and accompanied by Devaki-Vasudeva, Rohini, Uddhava and others, reached there but they also met their old relations from Vraja-kshetra (Mathura-Vrindavana-region). The Pandavas had also come with their wives and mother, Kunti. Devaki also met Kunti after a long time. Since both had suffered a lot, since they last met, tears welled up in both women's eyes.

While talking about the troubles Devaki said: "O Bhabi! Who could be as unfortunate as I had been, who couldn't see his son grow from infancy to maturity. I only learnt about his–Krishna's–childhood pranks and that captivating appearance from other people. I now greatly long to see Krishna in that form." Kunti said: " Don't worry. I will try to fulfil your wish."

Meanwhile, having learnt about Yashoda and Nanda Baba also reaching Kurukshetra, Krishna and Balarama couldn't keep themselves from running to the Vraja-Vasi camp. When Mother Yashoda heard about her 'Kanha's presence in Kurukshetra, she started asking everyone as to how she would be able to meet him. Madly she was asking all: "O bhai! Could you take this mother to her lost son? I would give you as many cows as you may demand from my stock. Oh......please help me."

At that very moment, she heard a faint note of the familiar tune being played on Bansuri. This made all the Gops assemble around and they were asking: "This is our Kannaiyah's flute. That tune is, unmistakeably the one we used to hear regularly, played on the bank of Yamuna! It means our Kanha is near!"

Then they heard much hustle and bustle of the coming chariots. Nanda Baba came and told Yashoda. "I got this message from Vasudeva that our Kanha is on his way to see us. Have you got some fresh navaneeta (butter) ready? He might demand it as the first thing. Also, have some misri (sugar candy) ready to mix it in butter. Balarama is also coming. I have aksed my men to prepare some thick rich milk. I know their preferences. Their childhood preferences never change."

Yashoda said: " I have enough stock."

Then there was much commotion and soon the old couple got the glimpse of the peacock feather and the saffron-yellow covering garment. Yashoda cried in ecstasy. "That is my Kanha!"

Then she heard the voice, her ears were longing to hear since ages: "Yes Maiyya! Here I am." And Krishna came and embraced his foster mother into an ecstatic union. In a trice, Krishna cast that impression before all the persons as if he was still a small boy clinging to his mother's bosom. All were spell-bounded to see that tear-jerking emotional reunion. Kunti had also reached there. As she beheld the unforgettable reunion, she immediately sent a chariot to bring Devaki there. In fact Devaki was already on her way. Half way, she met the messenger and reached there quickly. Kunti told her: "Bhabhi! See there! This is the form of your Krishna you longed to see. Have it to your eye-ful." And Devaki had her long cherished wish, fully fulfilled, seeing 'Kanha' in his 'Maiyya' Yashoda's lap. She could not check her tears and exclaim. "Real mother is the one who rears the child up and not the one who bears him!"

❏❏

# 42

# Arjuna Marries Subhadra

Shukadeva Ji said to Raja Parikshit: "O King! Now I tell you one interesting episode about your grandfather Arjuna."
Then he recounted the following story:--
Once while completing his pilgrimage to the western holy spots, Arjuna happened to reach Dwarika. Even otherwise, he sued to frequent Dwarika owing to his deep friendship with Lord Krishna. But this time when he reached there, he came to know about Balram's desire to marry off his sister Subhadra to Duryodhan, his (Balarama's) pet disciple whom he taught mace-fighting. Arjun also learnt that Krishna and his father Vasudeva, were not willing for this marriage. Adopting the guise of a brahmin recluse called Tridandi swami, he decided to remain in Dwarika, till the expiry of the rainy season.

When Balarama heard about a Tridandi Brahmin staying in Dwarika for the Chaturmas[1], he decided to invite the brahmin to his palace for learning the spiritual knowledge from him. But at the feast time, when Subhadra came there to serve them food, Arjuna in the guise of the brahmin, was bewitched by her incomparable beauty. Instantly he fell in love with Subhadra who had already developed a soft corner for Arjuna, knowing about his valour and prowess in archery from Krishna. Arjuna privately confided in Krishna about his decision and Krishna whole heartedly approved it. Then he made a plan. Subhadra was to go to a holy temple nearby, to complete her ritual worship of the Goddess Gauri. According to plan, Arjun reached there in a chariot arranged by Lord Krishna and quietly eloped with Subhadra, who was equally willing. They managed to hoodwink the soldiers escorting Subhadra. In order to help Arjun easily defeat the

---
1. **The four months of the rainy season.**

soldiers with his keen arrows, she had herself driven the chariot.

When the defeated soldiers reached near Balarama and told him about Arjuna's daring elopement with his sister Subhadra who appeared willing, Balram blew up: "How dare Arjuna challenge the honour of the Yadavs? Prepare an army and we'll teach him a lesson." But, Krishna pacified his brother. "You heard that Subhadra herself was willing. Even otherwise, she has learnt enough martial arts to defend herself and no body could have kidnaped her without her consent. So, instead of fighting Arjun, the scion of a very noble family and an ideal groom for our Subhadra, we had better go to him and duly solmenise the marriage."

All agreed. Balarama also realised the mistake, he was about to commit. Then he sent for the couple and duly solemmised the marriage.

□□

# 43

# A Strange Fact

It has been generally observed, that those whose chosen God is Lord Shankar, stay comparatively better off but those who concentrate their devotion on Lord Vishnu, are mostly poor and deprived of riches. This was also the query that rose in Raja Parikshit's mind and he put this before Shukadeva Ji.

Shukadeva Ji explained: "Lord Shiv is ever associated with his Shakti (the primal power). Lord Shiv is the presiding deity of all the three basic attributes. Sattavic, Rajasik and Tamasic tendencies. These attributes are theory of all Five Basic Elements, ten senses (five of the sense perception like sight, touch etc. and organs) and one mind (human). Even mastering one of them, one can get all the riches and perfections. But the Blessed (Lord Hari or Lord Vishnu) is beyond all these basic tendencies. Hence his devotees also transcend these humans yearningly. Once this question was also asked by Yuddhisthar. Answering it Lord Krishna said: "Those who come under my shelter are deprived deliberately by me, of all the deviations like riches, sensual delights, infatuative mortal relations etc, so that they may keep concentrating only on me. This way my devotees easily transcend all the moral hurdles[1], to merge their identity with that of

---

1. Curiously Enough, the Sundar Kanda of Goswami Tulsidas's 'RAMACHARITAMANAS' also puts similar views in Lord Rama's words. Lord Rama, while explaining to Vibhishan as to what kind of devotion appealed him most, says:
"Janani Janaka bandhu suta dhara
Tanu dhanu bhavan suhrida parivara
Sab kei mamata taag batoree
Mam padi manahi bandhi bari dori."
[Tie all the threads of affection to parents, brothers, sons and wives and of all the worldly comforts, riches etc. Into a big rope and bind your mind in that to devote your total attention to me.]

mine. While those, who seek other Gods' shelter get only what they desire and not final emancipation of the soul. In this sense, you may say it that I watch my devotee's interest better. But is not that I let them languish in poverty. I instil in them the sense, that they should not bother after temporary achievements. Hence, they themselves become indifferent to the objects of mortal delight."

Raja Parikshita was satisfied to get this explanation and he started worshipping Lord Supreme with doubled enthusiasm.

□□

# 44

# Devaki Gets Back Her Six Dead Sons

Devaki had lost six sons when her brother killed them at the time of their birth. When Krishna and Balarama returned from Kurukshetra, both Vasuedva and Devaki requested them hand-bound : "Now we are blessed with Blessed Lord incarnating as our sons. Our all desires stand, totally fulfilled. But we still long to meet our those six sons, your elder brothers, who were killed at the birth."

Hearing this request, Lord Krishna immediately summoned his Yogic powers to go to the 'Sutala Loka' [the realm where souls rest after losing their body]. Reaching there, he requested Bali, the lord of that realm to give him back those six children of Vasudeva and Devaki, and his elder brothers, to present them before their parents. Bali obliged and in no time, Krishna brought them back to Dwarika to present them before their parents. Devaki was thrilled to get back her lost sons. Even her breasts were filled up with milk in excessive affection.

This reunion not only fulfilled Devaki's cherished wish but also released those six souls from the bondage of a curse that they carried. Thus upon being released, they reached to the high realms due to them. Thus Lord Krishna made his parents filled with a beutiful contentment.

◫◫

# 45

## Bhasmasur Destroyed

Once Lord Shankar landed himself in a big trouble because of his nature to get propitiated easily and quickly. There was a demon called Vrikasur. He was a very powerful and robust person. Once he was advised by Narad: "Why don't you take some advantage of your robust health? You are quite powerful and only if you could get some boon from Lord Shankar, may be, you become the demon Lord!"

Narad sowed this seed of ambitions in Vrikasur's mind which made him a devotee of Lord Shankar. When he found Shiv not appearing before him even after years of his penance, he grew all the more determined to have the Lord before him. This time he started doing the worship of Lord Shankar in a typically demoniac manner. For six days he continued to hack off parts of his body and feed them to the raging fire of the altar. This all he was doing, to please Shankar, a Lord who easily thaws upon his devotees to offer them their desired boons at the mere expression of the wish. Then came the seventh day and the demon was about to hack off his head with a sharp edged axe, when Lord Shakar appeared before him, restricting by his hand, the hand of the demon he was about to strike at his own neck.

"Ask of your boon, devotee!" Lord Shaknar said.

Vrikasur said: "Grant me this boon that who-so-ever's head I place my hand upon should get incinerated to death."

Unmindfully Lord Shiv said: "So be it!" As soon as he got the boon, he rushed to place his hand on Shankar's head itself. Now, the Lord had not imagined such a terrible consequence, when he granted the boon. Since it was he who had given this boon, he couldn't have believed its effect. He appeared trapped in his own plot.

Lord Shiv had no go but to escape, with that demon, stretching his hand far ahead, in his trail. In fact the demon had his eye on beautiful Parvati, whom he wanted to marry after burning Shiva. While running fast, Shiva rushed to Vaikuntha, for he knew that it was only the Blessed Lord Vishnu, who could help him in the entire Universe. He quickly told Vishnu all that had transpired. Lord Vishnu couldn't help commenting: "O Great Lord! You have a very simple heart! You are really Bholenath!" But reassuring him, he further said: "Don't worry. You rest here till I take care of that 'Bhasmasur' with your boon!"

Lord Vishnu immediately adopted the form of a brahmin student and appeared before the demon, looking everywhere for Lord Shiva.

"Who are you searching for, Daityaraj?" the Blessed Lord asked.

The demon then told him about the power of burning anything by a mere touch of his hand that he had received from Shiv only. Having heard him, Vishnu laughed loudly: "Ha-Ha-Ha! You appear to have been duped by that half clad whimsical ascetic! I tell you, he has no such power to bestow such kind of boon. If you want to test his boon's efficacy, just place your hand upon your head.[1] I assure you, not even your hair would be burnt, let alone the whole body. Shiva is addicted to narcotic drugs and he himself doesn't know what he says."

Convinced by what Lord Vishnu had said, that demon casually put his hand upon his head. And lo and behold! he was incinerated to death.

---

1. **According to a different versions of this very story found in other sacred texts, Vishnu had adopted the form of a very beautiful dancer. While pretending to teach him (the demon) dance, Vishnu made the demon place his hand upon his own head which incinerated him to death instantly.**

# 46

## Who Among The Super Gods Is The Greatest?

Once all the great sages and seers assembled on the bank of the river Saraswati. While they were holding discussions among themselves, a debate started as to who among the super Gods, should be reckoned as the greatest. When the debate appeared unending, the wise sage Bhrigu was appointed to conduct a test on all the three Super Gods Brahma, Mahesh (Shiv) and Vishnu and apprise them of his conclusion.

Sage Bhrigu first went to Brahma's realm. Seeing his senior son, Brahma was delighted and came forward to lovingly embrace him. But Bhrigu responded with no matching expression. His behaviour enraged the Creator who blurted out: "You seem to have grown too arrogant ! Don't forget that I am the source of all of them." Without responding to him, the sage left the realm.

Then he reached the eternal abode of Lord Shankar. Seeing his brother[1] after a long time, Shiv came lovingly close to him. "Welcome, my brother!" Bhrigu arrogantly replied: "Don't call me your brother. You, an unclad fellow violating all norms of propriety, how can you claim any closeness with me? It is by mistake that I happened to come here. I now go back."

But Shiva was stung to the quick. He came charging at Bhrigu with his trident pointed at him. It was with much difficulty that Goddess Parvati could restrain him.

Then Sage Bhrigu reached Vaikuntha. At that time, the Blessed

---

1. Both Shiv and Bhrigu, according to the secred texts, had originated from Brahma's body and hence they were brothers.

Lord Vishnu was asleep. But not listening to whatever sentinels Lakshmi was saying, he straight away went to the Lord and hit him hard on the chest with his right leg.

Lord Vishnu woke up with a jerk and said in a supplicating voice: "O Great Sage! Your leg must have been hurt! Let me massage it." And saying so, Vishnu took the sage's leg in his lap. Sage Bhrigu was quite satisfied with Vishnu's noble behaviour. He immediately returned to the sages' assembly and declared: "Vishnu is the greatest, no doubt about it! No matter by God or Super God or a man, he who is considerate to his guests and who is devoid of all self conceited arrogance, is truly the Greatest."

The Super God, Lord Vishnu's greatness could be further judged by the fact that he always carries that footmark of the sage imprinted on is bosom!

◻◻

# 47

## Arjuna Purged of His Arrogance

Once in the court of Dwarika, there arrived a brahmin with the dead-bodies of his seven sons, who died as soon as they were born. Weeping bitterly, he accosted the entire court to register his complaint: "O Lord and the King and other stalwarts! The scriptures claim that the people of the state suffer a king's sins. Perhaps there is something wrong in the State-administration here, which has resulted in my seven sons' death. I condemn you all for this injustice that I am made to suffer."

Arjun happened to be present in that court when the Brahmin was condemning the rule of the state. He at once uttered: "How is it possible? Don't you have an able archer to provide adequate protection to this poor brahmin."

Whereupon, Lord Krishna advised Arjuna to take the charge to protect the Brahmina. But when Arjuna expressed his resolve to that brahmina, he said: "Why should I feel reassured with your this bow, when even Lord Krishna, Balarama and Pradyumna failed to protect my sons?"

This made Arjuna almost blow up in rage.

"O Brahmin Remember, I am not Krishna or Balarama but Arjuna, the wielder of the famous bow, Gandeeva. Now you go back to your home and come to me when your wife is about to deliver. Then I would guard your home with my Gandeeva and ensure no trouble to your next son." Arjuna assured the brahmina quite arrogantly and promised to end his life by jumping into the fire, should he fail to fulfill his vow.

At due time, the brahmin came back to Arjuna and Arjuna went to his home with his Gandeeva and arrow-full quiver ready. As he reached the home, he cast such a shield of his arrows around the brahmin's home that not even wind could have passed through it. As the time of delivery approached, Arjuna became all the more alert. Soon he heard the new-born child's cry but despite all the precautious the child disappeared into space, bodily. This made the brahmin extremely angry. He went straight to Lord Krishna and started condemning Arjuna for his vainglorious conceit "Your friend is hardly a man, let above be a warrior. He had bragged a lot about his powers but in reality he had none. My eighth son has also disappeared, right before his own eyes but he could do nothing!" This way the brahmin kept on censuring Arjuna.

Arjun was bewildered and stunned. But he decided to find out as to where that brahmin's son might have gone. Invoking his Yoga powers, he went to Yama's realm. Not finding him there, he visited all the realms of heaven and hell. But no where could he find that new born son. At last he returned dejected and according to his promise, began to enter into a burning fire to end his life. Then Lord Krishna explained to Arjuna: "Don't be so disappointed. Come along, I would show you where that brahmin's son could be."

Making Arjun seated in his wonderful chariot, he made it go towards west. As they kept on moving the chariot, they eventually managed to cross all the seven continents and then it entered a deep cave filled with pitched darkness. The darkness was so thick that the chariot's horse began to get confused and ran helter-skelter. Then Lord Krishna asked his wondrous discus, the Chakra Sudarshan to guide the way. That brilliant disc guided the chariot continuously till they went across that long dark cave. The realm, they had reached into was bright with a superb soothing glow. In ecstasy, Arjuna closed his eyes and the chariot went to the real fount of that light, placed upon wavy waters. The light had now become so dazzling, as to close the viewer's eye as if by reflex action. At last they reached an description defying palace, in which, lying upon his Serpent-Sesh's coil, was present no one else but Blessed Lord Vishnu himself. Narad was playing his luts and brahmin was singing his hymns. The Goddess of all propriety, Lakshmi, was massaging the Blessed Lord's feet.

Shri Krishna bowed to his yet another form, followed by Arjun. Both stood hand bound there. Then the Man Par excellence, the blessed Lord said. "Shree-Krishna-Arjuna, It was to seek your company, that I had made my Yogmaya to bring all the Brahma's (dead) sons here. Now you can return with all of them." Then addressing to both, the Blessed Lord said: "Krishna! I have incarnated in your form with my all the 16 potencies. Your life on the earth has a single objective: restoring the righteous order, slay all the demons and wicked people and lighten the burden of the earth. You both together, represent the mortal form of the clestial sages Nara-Narayana. Now taking the kids along with you return to finish your incomplete job."

When Arjun and Krishna returned the brahamin's all the eight boys, he was delighted to find them. Chanting Lord Krishna's glories, he returned home. Arjun was purged of his arrogance.

❏❏

# 48
# Lord Krishna Contemplates About Quitting the Mortal World

Once Narad, the divine sage, visited Dwarika and met Lord Krishna's father Vasudeva. Vasudeva said: "O Sage! I think my all wishes stand fulfilled since I could be the father of the Blessed Lord's incarnation in the Dwapar Age. But, do you think, that my soul will attain salvation now?" The sage replied: "Mortal wishes' fulfilment doesn't ensure salvation. Unless one devotes whole hearted to Lord Krishna's doings, one should may not attain salvation."

Giving this advice, Narad reached Lord Krishna's private chamber, which was accessible to all Gods, high sages and they could reach there any time. When Narad reached there, he found many Gods including Indra and Shiva present there. They all hymned the Lord in unison and then said : "O Great Lord! You are the sustainer of the entire Universe and you know every heart's secret. But now we have come to you with a specific request. We feel that the purpose of your incarnation has been achieved as you have established the righteous order. Now the advent of Kaliyug is round the corner. We request you to return to your eternal abode, Vaikuntha, as you have accomplished the job you were incarnated for. Now all your servants and devotees are praying for your return. Here in the world, your tales of the holy doings will sustain till you care to return as the Kalki Avataar. So, when do you plan to return to Vaikuntha?"

Smiling, the Lord said: "You are all very right . I have now established the righteous order in the mortal plane. I have lived in this mortal world for 125 years. Of course, my return to my eternal abode is due. But I am waiting for the sage's curse to become true.

He had rightly cursed the extermination of my clan. I also want it to happen, since my people are becoming increasingly delinquent and inequitous. Soon they shall perish through a self-destructing war. I don't want to leave the world till they are here. Their end is ordained. So, as soon as they perish, I shall return to my abode."

Meanwhile, a variety of natural disturbances had started taking place in Dwarika. All the seniors of the Yadava clan were worried. Uddhava, then sought refuge in Lord Krishna's counsel, who advised him.: "Worry not, Uddhava! No body can change the course of destiny. But till one is in the world, one should try to get the best from all entities, like Sage Dattetreya did."

❑❑

# 49

# The Twenty Four 'Gurus' of Dattatreya

We already know that Dattatreya was the son of Atri and Anusooya and according to Bhagwat, one of the incarnations of the Blessed Lord Vishnu. However, what distinguished him from other sages and seers, was his insight into nature and his capacity to learn various lessons from natural phenomena. Once while talking to King Yadu (the progenitor of the Yadav clan), he told him that one should try to make the best bargain out of what one received from one's Prarabdha (the consequence of the deeds performed in earlier lives). Recounting his twenty four Gurus (mentors or teachers), he mentioned the following names: Earth, Air, Sky, Water, Fire, Moon, Sun, Pigeon, Python, Sea, fire, flies, Bee, Honey bee, prostitute moulds Pingala, bird, a child, a virgin girl, the one who makes the arrows, fish and the bubble-bee. He said: "It is from them, that I take lessons and lead my life accordingly. Deem them as my saviours and my mentors." Then he started telling as to what lesson he learnt from each of them.

(1) **Earth:** It taught him how to be supremely patient and forgiving. While its trees and mounts told him, how to be useful to others–like giving shadow and protection, fruit and fresh air, and not demanding anything in return.

(2) **Air :** Air in the form of vital breath taught him, that one should partake of it at the bare optimum level, not a draught more or less. That is, one should bite only as much one could easily chew, not a morsel less or more. From the wind, he learnt how to touch every nook and corner of the world without showing any partiality to any one. Also, staying totally

uninfatuated by any one and keep constantly moving.

(3&4) **Water :** Water has no prejudice and takes the shape of the vessel it is poured in. Moreover, it teaches that water in the pitcher is not different from the water in a huge pond or ocean; similarly, soul in any individual is not different from the Supreme Spirit that pervades the whole of universe. He further claims, that an aspirant should be like clear sky. No matter there be a storm, or sun shine, clouds or moon shine, it remains untouched by all.

(5) **Agni :** An aspirant should be as bright as fire and nourishing (or helping to others) in moderate quality but devastating in large quantity. Meaning thereby, that an aspirant should be as much attached to world, as helps its growth. Since fire clandestinely remains in wood, the same way an aspirant should keep on doing good to others.

(6) **Moon :** Gives the lesson that though outwardly wanes and waxes, yet inwardly remains the same, so should be the spirit of an able aspirant, unchanged by external changes occuring in his life.

(7) **Sun :** It draws all superfluous moisture and excessive water from the earth's surface and returns it in the form of rain, when it needs them most. This way, it gives the lesson to the ascetics that they should indulge in the delights so as to be a part of the world but should leave them. Also, since it is one but is reflected in every water surface it touches upon, the same way God exists every where, though apparently in various receptacles (entities) yet it is one and the same.

(8) **The Pigeon :** Seeing the Pigeon, we must learn that one should never be bound by familial infatuations. Dattatreya says : "Once I spotted a pigeon couple, which also had tiny lings. One day, a hunter spread his net so far and wide that the pigeon-lings happened to be trapped into it. Seeing her children trapped, the

she pigeon felt so frustrated that she resignedly fell into that net. When the pigeon saw it, he felt so disappointed and forlorn that he also cried: "What is the purpose of staying in this world, when my dear wife is gone? So it is better that I also go her way and end my life. With the result, the entire pigeon family perished. So the pigeon teaches us, what we should never do. We should never be so frustrated to world bonds that we may lose our senses."

**(9)** **The Python :** This reptile teaches us that one should be content with whatever luck one is born with but still, never be weak and feel emaciated in whatever condition one has to live in.

**(10)** **The Sea :** The Sea teaches us (as opined by Dattartreya) how to be profound and unperturbed, no matter what be the external inputs. The sea never crosses its limits, no matter how much water is poured in it by the rivers or whatever moisture the sun takes away from it.

**(11)** **The Fire-Flies :** They teach us in a negative way, i.e. what should not be done by observing their effort and its consequence. One should never be so infatuated by any thing as to risk or even consume one's life, like what the fire-flies do.

**(12&13)** **The Bees or The Honey Bee :** They show the ideal way to the ascetics. Collect a bit of food from a variety of sources, so that you may have your need fulfilled without causing any burden upon any body. Hence, the recluse or the ascetic should not be dependent on one exclusive source to meet his requirement. This way, they can maintain their disaffection to anyone in particular but, at the same time, fulfil their needs as well. In this respect, the bubble-bee teaches us a great lesson. When repeatedly sitting on a lotus flower, it tries to stay there for a longer period, it gets imprisoned in it at the night-fall. Like a bee, one should keep on getting the essential virtues from various sources to develop them into the alternative sources for one self as well. The honey bee also teaches, how the elixir like honey, created by itself, is never consumed by itself. It is only meant for other's welfare.

(14) **The Elephant :** By observing a pachyderm's behaviour, we should learn what we shouldn't do. Driven by the sexual urge, it keeps on concentrating on the she-elephant to earn wrath of its other fellow beings. One should never get drawn by one's sensual urges or otherwise one lands one self into trouble. In fact, this lesson is for those, who have their vows disturbed by their sensual weaknesses.

(15) **The Primitive Originals (Bheela) :** We all must have seen the Bheels surviving on their trade of honey, which they steal from the honey-beehive. That is, one should never keep one's treasure of a long toil, so open otherwise it is likely to be stolen.

(16) **The Deer :** The deer's infatuation for sweet music teaches the ascetics that they should fight out their sensual weaknesses. The deer's weakness for melodious music, is repeatedly exploited to trap it into captivity. The hunter employ this trick to trace or even kill a deer. In this regard, the Shringi sage's example comes handy who, in his infatuation to sweet music, lost his all merit acquired to him out of decades of penance, in listening to the music played by the woman of easy virtue.

(17) **The Fish :** It gets enticed in the habit in the greed of getting the piece of the meat and loses its life eventually. So, it teaches us to stay clear from greed and infatuation which frequently become a cause of our doom.

(18) **The Prostitute, Pingala :** There was a beautiful prostitute named Pingala in Mithilanagari. Everyday in the evening, having adorned herself well, she used

to wait for a wealthy customer. Every potential customer appeared to her rich but as he came close, she would find him not as much rich as she would have liked. So she would reject him and wait for the other customer. This way, she passed many days in vain. At last, she developed aversion to her life: "How mean am I to keep myself immersed in this lowly trade." As she decided to get rid of her profession and live without expectation, she felt relieved. So her life taught Dattatreya, how to live in self contentment.

(19) **The Kurad Bird :** This bird is quite wise. When it finds other powerful birds assaulting it for the piece of meat held by him, it quickly throws it off to get relief from the assaulters. For Dattatreya, its lesson was, never to be greedy for something which might endanger one's life.

(20) **Children :** Dattatreya says children teach us lesson to derive self-contained happiness with the help of tiny playthings. A child is complete from within. Hence it enjoys bliss and sleeps for most of the time as all its pleasure sources lie within.

(21) **The Maiden :** Dattatrey says, that once he learnt about a maiden's supreme wiseness. One day, she received some guests when all her other relations were absent from the house. Those guests had come to choose the girl for one of their sons. But without getting nervous, she lovingly welcomed them. Then she asked them to wait and in the meantime, she began to prepare some dish for them. She never wanted to make any fuss about it. She had not much material for cooking so she started grinding the corn for preparing some dish. But while she did so, the bangles in the hands rattled a lot, giving the impression of their house's penury, which had nothing in store to offer to the guest. So, she put off her bangles, all but one and quietly ground the corn, without letting her guests know anything

about that destitute household. Dattatreya says that the maiden's wiseness to put off all her bangles, teaches us that the real knowledge is acquired in loneliness.

(22) **The one who moulds the arrow-blades :** Says Dattatreya, that this person taught him how to concentrate on the job at hand. A little carelessness on his part might ruin all the arrows. Giving one example he says, that once an arrow-blade maker was busy in his job and his king, with his entire retinue passed from that road. But unaware of that pomp and show he kept on making the arrow blades. The king also praised him for his deep concentration.

(23) **The Snake :** It teaches us to work quietly and clandestinely to achieve its aim. Snakes never move in herd, when taking revenge from their assailant. The same way, a Yogi must move alone without any procession of followers behind him.

(24) **The Spider :** Dattatreya says that a spider acts like God. It issues saliva from its mouth, creates its web out of it and then eats it back. The same way, God creates the world and destroys it to send it back into himself. The bubble bee, he further says, makes the insect acquire its own form, once it is trapped by it. The same way, he, who goes to God becomes a part of God himself.

Concluding his sermons, Dattatrey told Raja Yadu that this way, he had drawn lessons from various entities. The idea is, that nothing is worthless in the world only if one has an idea to make the best use of them.

Referring to this Avadhootapakhyan, Lord Krishna advised Uddhava that he should also follow this superior knowledge to get over his worldly infatuations and temptations.

◻◻

# 50

# The Details About Lord Krishna's Family

When troubled by Jarasandha's repeated attacks on Mathura, Shri Krishna decided to shift his clan's abode from there to Dwarika. He faced many objections to his proposal. It was natural, that the clan living for generations at that particular place should oppose it. But when Krishna explained the logic behind his suggestion of mass migration to Dwarika, they, willingly agreed.

It was, actually a huge clan containing as many as 100 families. Shri Krishna's personal family, was quite big. He had eight queens and 16,000 other queens, who were actually the women having no shelter and he provided them a safe place to live honourably in. They were the women he had released from the lecherous demon Narkasur's captivity.

Shri Krishna, by his deed, thought and action had shown the ideal way of staying in the family. The Srimad Bhagwat claims, that the number of his sons, grandsons, great grandsons born on both paternal and maternal side, was more than 10 million. He had 18 valorous and brilliant sons. Among them some of whose names were Pradyumna, Aniruddha, Deeptiman, Bhanu, Samba, Madhu, Vrishabuham, Chitrabhanu, Viroop, Kavi, Nayagrodha etc. Pradhumna was the eldest among them and the most competent. Aniruddha, the grandson had the power equivalent to that of 10,000 elephants. Aniruddha had married Narayana's grand daughter and this union had produced, Vajranabha, the sole survivor in the clan, following the sage's curse that virtually effaced this clan through an internecine feud among its members. The Srimad Bhagwat claims, that to impart education to the boys of this clan, there were millions of (the figure quoted is 3 crore 88 lakh) teachers. Hence, it is difficult to count the exact number of students. It is claimed that, when the Blessed Lord decided to incarnate himself as Lord Krishna, he asked most of the 33 crore Gods to take birth on the earth at the same time.

But as the destiny would have, despite all these happy and prosperous families, the Yadava clan couldn't survive and perished due to a sage's curse, which has been explained ahead. However, Lord Krishna had realised it that his clan's days on the earth were numbered. In fact he had been advised by the astrologers as well that he should leave Dwarika as it might be submerged by the ocean. It was on Krishna's advice, that his clan people had gone to Prabhas-kshetra. It was an auspicious spot, where in the Satyayug, Daksha, the Progenitor, had recovered from the deadly disease of tuberculosis, by staying in this region's holy and healthy climate.

But exactly when all the Yadavs were preparing to go to Prabhas-Kshetra, Uddhava quietly came to Lord Krishna, realising the Lord's intention of quitting his mortal coil. He supplicated privately before the Lord : "O Lord! Please don't leave us. We have become so used to living in your company, that we may not survive without you. Hence if you plan to quit, please take us along."

Then Lord Krishna told him, how he could be realised even, when not physically present. Reassuring Uddhava, the Lord said: "I am present in every bit of the creation. You have to take inspiration from nature to realise me in my absence, as Dattatreya did. Then he narrated the 'Avadhoota pakhyan', centring on Dattatreya's getting knowledge from nature, which has already been discussed in the previous story.

❏❏

# 51

# The End of the Yadava Clan

When the war of Mahabharat ended making the Pandavas as the eventual winners, they visited Hastinapur with Lord Krishna to meet their mother Kunti, and condole the death of all the Kauravas with their (Kaurava's) parents Dhritarashtra and Gandhari. But, as Lord Krishna bowed to show his respect to Gandhari, the mother of the Kauravas, she thundered : "Krishna! You alone could have checked this catastrophical war but you didn't . So I curse you that as you have seen the Puru dynasty almost perish totally, the same shall be the fate of your clan as well."

Lord Krishna, head-bowed, accepted the curse and said: "O Grand Lady! Your curse is also pre-ordained. I know I have to witness that tragic end of my clan as well."

After formally appointing Maharaja Yuddhisthar the king of Hastinapur, Lord Krishna left for Dwarika.

The conditions in Dwarika were also not good. Owing to Krishna's prolonged absence, his clan people had grown quite delinquent and tyrant. Moreover, in order to avoid siding with any warring group in Mahabharat, Balarama had gone on a long pilgrimage. With the result, there was no controlling authority in Dwarika. With no check on their delinquency and lots of wealth available, Lord Krishna's family members, sons, grandsons, cousins etc.–had ceased to be virtuous. They had all grown addicted to various drugs and dirty habits. The Mahabarat war, had also created dissatisfaction in their rank and files. They would tolerate no interference in their villainous pranks. Often they would fight with their fellow cousins. On returning to Dwarika, Lord Krishna was quite unhappy seeing their rowdy behaviour.

Once the youth of Yadav clan tried to fool a learned sage, by showing him a male disguised as a pregnant lady. Then they asked him as to what 'she was going to beget'. The sage, seeing through their artifice, grew very angry and cursed that the product of 'this lady' would spell doom for the entire clan of Yadu. The male disguised as female was no one but Krishna's own son Sambha, from Rukmini. No doubt, he was a bad son. However, following that curse, when they opened Sambha's clothes, they really found an iron club inside. In panic they pounded it to dust and threw it into the sea. But the dust returned to the shore and grew into the bushes that bordered the land. It is claimed that the bushes and reed had grown so thick, as to be converted into handy swords and spears. However, one piece of that iron club could not be reduced to powder form and a fish swallowed it. Subsequently the fish was caught and the iron piece was taken out to form the blade of an arrow. It was this blade which, later on, pierced Lord Krishna's sole as he lay resting.

When Krishna returned from the Mahabharat war, he was forewarned by the astrologers that Dwarika was doomed. Dreadful convulsions had began to shake the earth. Seeing all these symptoms signifying the onset of the Kaliyug, Krishna advised his people to behave properly and cease drinking wine etc.

One day, however, all the Yadavas assembled on the sea-shore in Prabhas-kshetra to celebrate a festival. On that day, they were allowed to drink wine. But after drinking intoxicants they became so much quarrelsome, as to start hitting each other recklessly. Soon their celebration turned into a war. Indiscriminate killing took place, with most of them using that very reed as the weapon till every one was slain and the whole of the Yadavas clan was totally destroyed.

The only survivors were Krishna and Balarama, who resignedly left for a quiet spot on the shore of the sea. Thus curse of Gandhari and of the sage had come true.

❏❏

# 52

# Lord Krishna Departs For His Eternal Abode

When Lord Krishna saw his elder brother Balarama sitting on the shore of the sea and a white huge snake emerging from his mouth and vanishing into the ocean, he realised that his brother has coalesced his spirit with the Supreme Spirit[1]. Sadly he went inside the dense jungle closely, reclined against a tree and resignedly thought that his stay over the earth was drawing to a close. As he thought of quitting his mortal coil, his body suddenly started glowing with a brilliant dazzle. He was lying down on the flat earth with his one (right) leg resting on the knee of the other. From a distance his reddish sole gave the impression, as though a tiny deer was sitting on a yellowish bush. A hunter, who happened to be not far off, thought it to be a tiny deer and shot his arrow, aiming at the Lord's raised sole. The blade of this arrow had been wrought by the same piece of iron, which had led to the virtual extermination of the Yadava clan in an intra-racial feud.

When the hunter came close to his 'prey', he was shocked to see his arrow embedded into the Lord's sole. At once, he realised his mistake and requested the Lord, hand bound: "Kill me this very moment, O Lord, for having hit you with an arrow. Slay me, please!"

But reassuring him, the Lord (Krishna) said: "It's not your fault. This was destined to happen. It is my will. In the earlier age, you were Bali, the brother of Sugriva, and I was Rama. Since I had shot you dead without any provocation from your side, I did feel sorry and willed that in this age, our scores should be settled. Now don't worry, for you have acted according to my will." As the hunter learned about his

---

1. A different version of the Purana claims that at his end a brilliant beacon had emerged from balaram's mouth and had unified with Lord Krishna's existence.

earlier existence, he recollected the incident. Exactly then an aerial vehicle from the heaven landed there and after reverentially circumanlulating around the Lord, it escorted that hunter to heaven.

Meanwhile, searching for his Lord, Daruka, the Lord's chariot-driver, happened to reach there, guided by the inimitable fragrances of the Lord's fallen Vaijayant garland. Coming down from the chariot, Daruka bowed to him. As he left the vehicle, it along with the horse and weapons flew away to heaven.

Daruka started crying seeing the Lord so quite and forlorn. "Don't cry Daruka, for this was all that was destined to happen. Now you should go back to Dwarika and tell my grand parents, Rohini and King Ugrasen about my and Balaram, finally quitting our mortal forms. Tell them to quit Dwarika, too, and go to Indraprastha with Arjun whom you'd give this message. When I am gone, this sea would submerge Dwarika. And when you have done this duty, concentrate on my form to leave this world as well."

A totally desolate and melancholic Daruka left for Dwarika. Getting the hint about the Lord's interns, in Vaikuntha all Gods assembled to welcome Lord back to his eternal abode. Meanwhile, on the Earth, the Lord so quietly quitted his mortal coil, that nobody could know. And alongwith him to his realm truth went, righteousness, kindness, glory and all auspicious prosperity.

As the message reached Dawrika, all of them became very sad and grief-stricken. Immediately they all rushed to the coast but fell flat on to the earth, severely wailing in sorrow. Devaki-Vasudeva quickly died. Most of the women had consumed themselves on the pyre of their dead husbands. Arjun had reached there by this time. He took along the remaining women and Lord Krishna also realised, that now there was no purpose of his staying in the active world. Making Vajranabh the king of Mathura, and appointing Parikshit the King of Hastinapur, the Pandavas also left for the Himalayas with their common wife Draupadi and one by one, they all also quitted their body to be with the Super Lord, leaving the trail of an inexhaustible glory of their deeds performed under Lord Krishna's direction. By this time Kaliyug had completed 36 years of its stay on the earth.

# 53

# The Dynasties In Kaliyug

When the crown-jewel of the dynasty of Yadu, Lord Krishna, quitted his mortal coil and left for his eternal abode, Vaikuntha, the earth was, subsequently ruled by the following dynasties, as are briefly described in the Srimad Bhagwat.

The last ruler in the lineage of Jarasandha's father Varihadrath, will be king Ripunjaya. But his minister, Shunak shall kill him and appoint his own son as the king. This dynasty shall also have five rulers, who shall rule for 138 years. Then the king will be Shishunaga and his dynasty's 10 rulers will rule over the earth, for 360 years in the Kali Age. The next ruling dynasty will be the one started by Mahapadma Nanda. He shall be a powerful tyrant and shall cause the destruction of many small rulers. It is from his rule, that the kings will acquire irreligious attitude and will start behaving like the Shoodras.

Mahapadma Nanda shall have eight sons who shall rule subsequently. But during this dynasty's rule, shall emerge a brahmin with the name Kautilya or Chanakya, who shall cause death to all the eight sons of Nanda. Then Chanakya would make Chandra Gupta Maurya as the king. Ten rulers of this dynasty shall rule. Then the military commander, named Pushyamitra shall kill his king to become the ruler himself. His dynasty will be called Shunga which will have 10 rulers.

The Shunga dynasty will be replaced by the Kanva dynasty which shall be of brahmin class. The king of this dynasty will be less virtuous than the earlier kings. The last Shunga ruler will be Devahooti, who shall be a cruel person. He will kill the king Vasudeva of the Kanva dynasty and become himself the king. The four rulers of Kanva dynasty shall rule for 354 years. Their last king, Sushama, shall be killed by his Shoodra servant, who will himself rule. Then his brother shall rule. These 30 kings shall be ruling over the earth for as many as 456 years.

Then after, the earth shall be ruled by Aabheera Gardhabhi and Kanak dynasties, followed by the ruler of the Yavana and Turks. As the Kaliyug intensifies its influence, the rulers of Saurashtra, Avanti, Aabheera, Hara, Ambud, Kaal and other kingdoms will be without noble, brahaminical virtues. Even the king will start behaving like the lowly Shoodras. Right from the bank of the river Sindhu, to the coastal regions along the river Chandrabhaga, Kauntipuri and entire Kashmir will fall under control of the Malechcha and those brahmins who would be without the noble, brahminical virtues. They shall all be wicked by nature and would not hesitate in killing, even the noble brahmins, women and children. They won't feel shy in looting others' property and women. There will be no sacred, traditional 'samskaras' (noble virtues) and these kings will bleed their people like the savage, Maleecha kings. Eventually, they shall all perish due to their own misdeeds and inhuman acts.

Shukadeva advised Raja Parikshit: "Remember King! Time is the most powerful ruler. As the Kaliyug spreads its fangs, the righteous order, piety, kindness, power of memory all will wane gradually. The evil will get the best services, while the virtuous, religious people will starve. In fact the lesser be the man, the greater honour will he command. He shall be deemed eminently successful. The brahmins will wear the sacred thread only for the sake of it, without following any of the rules associated with it. There will hardly be noble persons, those who may exist will maintain a sham behaviour. Only the cheaters and impostors among them, shall be considered greater noble persons. Corruption will be rampant even in judiciary and justice will become a purchasable commodity. For serving their lowly, selfish ends, the people will sue faith and religion. They will only be tools to gain greater renown or notoriety. The Earth will experience severe droughts and natural calamities. Many deadly, incurable diseases will surface. Human life span will be sustaintially reduced. The impostors will take hold of the religious places.

The guests shall be ill-treated. When morality touches its lowest, then 'Kalki' incarnation will take place. The Blessed Lord Vishnu shall appear in the form of a boy 'Kalki' in a noble brahmin Vishnuyasha's home in a small village called Sambhala. Then, for the preservation of the righteous order and the decline of the iniquitous reign, the Lord, with a keen sword in his hand, astride a horse named Devadutta, shall kill the wicked and rogues."

Shukadeva further said: "Kaliyug had commenced when the Sun, Moon and Jupiter had together entered the Pushya constellation; at the time the Saptarshi (the seven Sages Ursa Major) will also enter the Magha constellation. However, again when the Sun, the Moon and Jupiter re-enter the first phase of Pushya Nakshatra (constellaton) the Satyayug will start. Kaliyug is likely to last for 4,32,000 years. When the sun transited from Magha to Poorvashada Nakshatra, the Kaliyug assumed its full charge, leading to Nanda getting installed as the king."

It is claimed in Srimad Bhagwat that two brothers of king Shantanu (Grandsire Bheeshma's father), Divapi and Maru still dwell in a village called Kalashi and they would help the Blessed Lord revive the righteous order in the Kalki incarnation. Hence, till the time that period dawns, all should devote themselves to Lord Krishna's devotion to survive this decadent and disturbing world.

Then Raja Parikshit wanted to know from Shukadeva as to which are the symptoms to be heard for the advent of Kaliyuga, and how could one get above them.

Shukadeva said: "O King! Most of them have been enumerated by me but the one who devotedly chants Lords Krishna's name, gets rid of all the troubles caused by Kaliyuga. In Satyayug, one could get better status of one's rigorous penance; in Treta by performing massive Yagyas, in Dwapar by ritually worshipping Lord Krishna. But in Kaliyug the only redemption one could get from the deadly sins and impious acts, is by religiously singing the glories of Lord Krishna. For the people of Kaliyug, the succour is only enchanting Lord Krishna's name. That's what you should also do as the Kaliyug has already set in."

◻◻

# 54

# The Description of The Final Dissolution or *Pralaya*

Brahma's one day equals a Kalpa or 1000 cycles of the four Ages (Satya, Treta, Dwapar and Kaliyug). After every Kalpa, the final dissolution takes place for a similar duration. Having ordained the period of each Age, Brahma appears in the form of Rudra. At the end of a thousand cycles of the four ages, the Earth's most part is exhausted. A total death then ensues, which lasts a hundred years and in consequence of the failure of food all beings become languid and at last entirely perish. The eternal Vishnu, then assumes the character of Rudra, the destroyer, and descends to reunite all his creatures with himself. He enters into the seven rays of the Sun, drinks up all the water of globe, and causes all moisture, whatever, in living bodies or in the soil, to evaporate, thus drying up the whole earth. The seas and rivers, the mountain-torrents, and springs are all exhausted, and so are all the waters of Patal, vapourised by the fire poked out by Serpent Shesh.

The great fire, when it has burnt all the 'Lokas' of Patal, proceeds to the death and consumes this also. A vast whirlpool of flame then spreads to the region of the atmosphere and the realm of Gods, and wraps them in ruins. The three spheres show like a frying pan amidst the surrounding flames, that prey upon all moveable and stationary things.

The inhabitants of the two upper spheres, having discharged their functions, are being annoyed by the heat. When they become heated, its tenants, who after the full period of their stay, are desirous of ascending to higher regions, depart from the Janaloka (the realm of the devotees). Those saintly mortals, who had diligently worshipped

Vishnu and are distinguished for piety, abide at the time of dissolution in Maharloka, with the Pitras (progenitors), the Manu and the seven Rishis, the various orders of celebratial spirits and Gods. These, when the heat of the flames that destroyed the world reach Maharloka, repaid to Janaloka in their subtle form, destined to become re-embodied in similar capacities as their former, when the world is renewed, at the begining of the succeeding Kalpa. This continues throughout the life of Brahma, at the expiration of his life all are destroyed, but those who have by then attained a residence in the Brahmaloka, by having identified themselves in spirit with the supreme, are finally resolved to the sole existing Brahma. Janaradan (Vishnu or Krishna) in the form of Rudra, having consumed the whole world, breathes forth heavy clouds. Mighty in size and loud in thunder, they cover all space. Showering down torrents of water, these clouds quench the dreadful fires which involve the three worlds, and then they rain without interruption for a hundred years and deluge the whole universe. Pouring down in drops as large as a hen eggs, these rains spread the earth, and fill the middle region and heaven. The world is now enveloped in darkness, and all things inanimate and animate, having perished, the clouds continue to pour down water for more than a hundred years.

Then again peace returns, waters begin to subside. The Supreme Spirit, in the form of Krishna (or Vishnu) reigns. And from this primal deity, emerges the pristine lotus having Brahma placed in it. And then, Brahma restarts the process of creation by planting life, given in the 'matter' of the earth. Thus the evolution of life is again set in motion, to travel through various Palaezoic and Mesozoic times; from the fish living in water, to the tortoise. Then through the Cenozoic time, where it passes from the boar to the man-lion, half human and half animal till it reaches the fully human stage; the dwarf, followed by the first human hero (Parashuram), the first perfect man (Rama) to the perfect being (Lord Krishna). So the cycle continues ceaselessly, without end.

◻◻

# 55

# Raja Parikshit's Salvation And Janmejaya's 'Naag-Yaga'

While concluding the recitation of the Holy Purana, Srimadbhagwat, Sage Shukadev impressed upon Raja Parikshit: "O King! Now I have recited before you the whole of Srimad Bhagwat which essentially contains the details of Lord Krishna's wonderful life.

"Realise that Shree Hari is Lord Krishna, who is no different from Brahma or Shiv. Now, having listened to it, you must not fear death. Death is nothing but change of bodies for the soul, like a body itself changes its clothes. The body is doomed to perish, since it is the soul that is immortal. It is the elemental form of the Supreme Spirit which permeates every bit of universe. Soul doesn't perish with the end of the world either. Now with your discretionary sense, you must meditate on God's Immortal Form, for therein lies your soul's salvaton. Coalesce with him. Then Takshak will be able to sting only your body. So, fear not O King!"

Having listened to the Great Srimad Bhagwat, as interpreted by Saint Shukadeva, Raja Parikshit's fear and remorse vanished. Gratefully he bowed to Shukadeva Ji and said : "O Great saint! Now I have no fear in my heart! I know that this whole Universe is instict with Lord Krishna's Immortal Spirit. Death and Life are occasional halts on the path, that the soul traverses. Now all my ignorance stands removed."

After this, Raja Parikshit reverentially bade adieu to Shukadeva and prepared himself to leave this mortal world.

Meanwhile, Taksaka, the king serpent, prepared himself for the task that sage Shringi had bidden him for. As he was on its way, he suddenly met a brahmin boy, named Kashyapa. On enquiry, he learnt that Kashyapa was an expert in devising anti-dose for the snake-bite. Kashyapa said: "I have heard that the snake-lord Takshaka is coming to fatally sting my king Parikshit. But I'd see to it that my king doesn't die of that snake-bite." Since Takshaka was in disguise of a brahmin, Kashyapa couldn't identify him. Hearing Kashyap's challenge, Takshaka appeared in his original form and said: "I'm Takshaka. Let me test your prowess. Now I bite this green tree." As he did so, that green tree was reduced to a dry and withered tree due to the high toxicity of the bite. Kashyapa chanted a Mantra and sprinkled some water on that withered tree. Lo and behold! It was green again. Takshaka realised that he won't be able to make Shringi's curse true, if this brahmin stayed near Parikshit. He lured the brahmin with lots of gold, taking which Kashyap agreed to return. Having cleared this obstacle, Takshaka reached Raja Parikshit's palace and bit him fatally to end the king's life.

When, Parikshit's son, Janmejaya learnt about Takshaka killing his father, he asked his priest Dhaumya, to arrange a Yagya in which all the snakes of the world might be incinerated to death. Soon the Yagya was arranged and the priests started chanting the holy mantras to suck all the snakes into the holy pit of fire. With their every chant of 'Swaha', herds of snakes began to be sucked by that deadly fire. But Takshaka, the main target of Janmejaya, couldn't be sucked. On being asked, the priests told Janmejaya that Takshak had hidden himself beneath the throne of Indra. "Chant such a mantra which may force Takshaka to be sucked into the holy pit along with Indra's throne." The sages chanted the Mantra and soon Indra on his throne, with Takshaka wrapping himself around the throne's legs were visible in the sky. Both of them would have fallen in the fire, but for Brahma's intervention. He advised Janmejaya: "King! It is unfair to destroy a whole species out of sheer vengeance. Your father met his death when his time in this world was over. All die, in accordance with the time scheduled by Providence. Takshaka was only an instrument, to cause it happen in your father's case. So stop this cetestrophical Yagya."

By the time sage Asteeka, the nephew of the Snake-Lord, Vauki, also reached the venue. He chanted a counter spell to make Takshaka stay in the heaven and prevent his fall into the holy fire. Heeding to the Creator's advice, Janemjaya also asked the priests and sages to stop the Yagya, and let the other snakes survive. In any case Janmejaya had avenged his father's death by threatening the whole species of snakes.

❏❏

# DIAMOND POCKET BOOKS PRESENTS
## SHIRDI SAI & RELIGIOUS BOOKS

**B. Umamashwara Rao**
- *The Spiritual Philosophy of Shri Shirdi Sai Baba Shirdi ... 150.00
- *Sri Shirdi Sai Baba ... 60.00
- *Thus Spake Sri Shirdi Sai Baba ... 40.00

**Dr. S.P. Ruhela (Com. & Ed.)**
- *The Immortal Fakir of Shirdi ... 150.00
- *Sai Grace and Recent Predictions ... 95.00
- *The Divine Glory of Shri Shirdi Sai Baba ... 150.00 [Experience of Devotees in the Post-Samadhi Period (1918-1997)]
- *Shirdi Sai : The Supreme ... 80.00
- *Divine Grace of Sri Shirdi Sai Baba ... 150.00
- *Divine Revelations of a Sai Devotee ... 50.00
- *Sri Shirdi Sai Bhjanavali (In Roman) ... 30.00

**Chakor Ajgaonkar**
- *The Footprints of Shirdi Sai .. 100.00
- *Tales from Sai Baba's Life ... 60.00

**B.K. Chaturvedi**
- *Sai Baba of Shirdi ... 60.00

**Sushila Devi Ruhela**
- *Sri Shirdi Sai Bhajanmala (Roman) ... 10.00

**D.K. Chaturvedi**
- *Gods & Goddesses of India ... 150.00
- *Shiv Puran ... 75.00
- *Vishnu Puran ... 75.00
- *Shrimad Bhagvat Puran .. 75.00
- *Devi Bhagvat Puran ... 75.00
- *Garud Puran ... 75.00
- *Agni Puran ... 75.00
- *The Hymans & Orisons of Lord Shiva (Roman) ... 30.00
- *Sri Hanuman Chalisa (Roman) ... 30.00
- *Pilgrimage Centres of India ... 95.00

**S. K. Sharma**
- *The Brilliance of Hinduism ... 95.00
- *Sanskar Vidhi (Arya Samaj) ... 95.00

**Dr. B.R. Kishore**
- *Hinduism ... 95.00
- *Rigveda ... 60.00
- *Samveda ... 60.00
- *Yajurveda ... 60.00
- *Atharvveda ... 60.00
- *Mahabharata ... 60.00
- *Ramayana ... 60.00
- *Supreme Mother Goddesses Durga (4 Colour Durga Chalisa) ... 95.00

**Manish Verma**
- *Fast & Festivals of India .. 95.00

**Manan Sharma**
- *Buddhism (Teachings of Buddha) ... 95.00
- *Universality of Buddha ... 95.00

**Anurag Sharma**
- *Life Profile & Biography of Buddha ... 95.00
- *Thus Spake Buddha ... 95.00

**Udit Sharma**
- *Teaching & Philosophy of Buddha ... 95.00

Order books by V.P.P. Postage Rs. 20/- per book extra. Postage free on order of three or more books, Send Rs. 20/-- in advance.

## DIAMOND POCKET BOOKS (P) LTD.
X-30, Okhla Industrial Area, Phase-II, New Delhi-110020.
Phones : 51611861- 65, Fax : (0091) -011- 51611866